Protection That Can't Be Beat

My Bible Diaries
Psalm 91 Blessing

Tarshish Productions
Elkhart, Indiana

Linda C. Newberry

Published by Tarshish Productions, 1933 N Stone Maple Lane, Elkhart, Indiana 46514.

Unless otherwise noted, Scripture quotations are taken from the King James Bible.

References to Strong's concordance are taken from the Strong's Exhaustive concordance in both book and electronic form.

Dictionary definitions mentioned are from MacMillan and WordNet online Dictionary's

ISBN 978-1-941201-02-2

www.lindacnewberry.com
Printed in the United States of America

Table of Contents

Acknowledgements

Thank you to the group of business associates, friends and family who have been a part of my weekday Bible study email. I have had many emails over the last several months telling me that in one way or another these word studies of verses have helped you to understand His meaning better, or that something in the study or prayer has hit a particular chord in whatever your current circumstance was, or just thanking me for opening this weekday study to you. Prior to the email I did my study in the form of journaling. This email started by sending off one of my daily studies as something to help a couple of my associates and now has morphed into something much larger.

What you may not know is the blessing it has been to me to be able to have a structured daily responsibility in providing these expanded verses, my musings and then a prayer to open the day. After spending well over the normal 40-50 hours a week during a 40+ year career and then being side-lined with physical difficulties, it has been a healing balm for me to know in a very real way that it is still possible to be effective and useful to people in my circle.

Thank you from the bottom of my heart.

Introduction

Welcome to My Bible Diaries!

Studying extensively is something I have done from almost my first moment as a Christian. My life was about as messy as it could get. Years of not understanding who I was or who I belonged to, created many wrong thought processes and thereby, speech patterns and actions that weren't worthy of a child of God.

One of the first gifts God gave me was an understanding that I needed more, a lot more, wisdom….and a hunger to find it. I was without work then, and I was offered a temporary position for several months. I was able to complete the work necessary within two to three hours but they still needed me there to answer the phones for the rest of the day. I asked if it would be okay to study my Bible during those five to six hours per day as long as I didn't let the reception duties slide and they happily agreed. Interesting, to say the least, considering they were not openly Christian folks. Thank you God!

There were other situations that engrained in me the need to study as a daily habit. The study convinced me of the importance of focused thinking and changing my speech patterns to include confessing right words. This carried through even when I worked full-time (although in-depth scripture study was a bit more sporadic), this study continued on a weekly basis.

I have been doing this in excess of twenty years now and continue to find new and exciting nuggets of God's gold. Recently I have had some physical issues that have brought me home from corporate America. I did not want to sit and wallow, which is especially easy to do when your body doesn't feel well. I wanted to continue to be of use. Although I was close to retirement age, it was still several years off. As much as we all talk about how great it will be once we aren't working, all people who go from 150 mph in the corporate setting to 1-10 mph find themselves wrestling with many questions about their new relevance in life and to humanity.

Relevance at work, in your position is easy to gage. Corporations are centered in measurable results and if you are good at what you do you have results that folks can see. However you come home after working for 40+ years and you find that most of your work friends don't call or come over. Some are uncomfortable. They don't know what to say. It becomes necessary to actively plan this new existence. You quickly find that you are and probably have been all along, responsible for finding your relevance while in my case caring for my body....and in your case caring for your family or career or when you are done with your career, the massive change from a 40+ hour week to the new frightening and exciting phase of retirement.

Healing takes time. In this situation a lot more time than I have wanted. Two to three hours of what I now call up time is what I have to offer, however my ability to do much physically is still severely limited. Setting aside upset about my external circumstance and choosing to look at this differently was important for me to move ahead.

One day a particular study I was working on had some nuggets I thought a couple of my friends could use to brighten their day. Their response was positive. So as I reached out to family/friends and ex-coworkers and associates over the next few months, I began to ask if they would be interested in joining our little weekday business person's study. Week by week the list grew. This weekday Bible study email has now turned into blog posts. This has become an avenue for me to keep in touch with many of my business associates, friends and now new followers and Facebook fans.

Neither you nor I will ever be at a point in our development to set aside study. The studies in this collection are meant to give you food for thought. They are not meant for full explanation and frankly, if I were to study them over again today there would be new nuggets that would come out. When you see the definitions and the verse, you will see more than what his written. You should expect that. It is one of the beauties of God's word. Depending on the time of life and things you are dealing with, different aspects of the verse will show itself.

These are verses or series of verses that have been used in my own life as confessions to change my circumstances, bringing my life to more closely resemble the life God had planned out for me. He paints vivid pictures of our health, our relationships (with Him and with others), our spiritual and emotional being, our social standing, our political leanings and….our life work, financial and material status. My hope is that you will find in these studies the reason and means to stand firm until you see change into that God vision designed just for you. These are studies that can and should be read over and over, used in Bible studies and mulled over in prayer time….this is not a one show pony.

The layout for the study starts with the chosen verse showing in parentheses the key definitions from the Strong's Concordance and/or extended definitions from the dictionary when needed; next my study and prayer for your day; finally you will find the full Strong's definition, followed by any root words associated with the word studied. The reason I am showing you these is that as I continue to be astounded at some of these definitions, I expect that you will be also. I do not want you to think I am just making this stuff up. That's how good it is!

You may ask, 'How can you promote this when you have a real and present health need yourself?' My answer is that my belief in healing is no less now than before I became afflicted, and I need these words more now than ever. I will continue to read and study....become more focused in my thinking and speech no matter what seems to be going on around me. I am not done yet! And neither are you!

Enjoy these studies and please feel free to contact us at info@lindacnewberry.com

We look forward to hearing from you.

CHAPTER 1

Fear, Your Protection From It

Psalm 91:1 (KJV)

1 He that dwelleth (<u>sits down, remain, settle in, tarry, inhabit</u>) in the secret (<u>a cover, hiding place, privily: confidentially or in secret, protection</u>) place of the most High (<u>the Supreme, ascend up, increase, perfect, prefer, raise, recover, restore</u>) shall abide (<u>to stop over night, stay permanently, be obstinate in words, dwell, endure, remain, tarry</u>) under the shadow (<u>defence, through the idea of hovering over, an opaque object, a representative figure, image</u>) of the Almighty (<u>to be burly-muscular, strong, and heavy built, powerful, impregnable-well protected, unable to be taken by storm</u>).

As Christians, we are told "Fear not...." one hundred and forty-four times in the Word. The more we keep the Word of God in our eyes, mind, and mouth; the more peace we will be able to walk in. It is a time in history as most of us have never seen in our lives.

There have been other times when folks said that our earth was in a position for the Second Coming. But, according to the events that need to happen before Jesus' return, we can clearly see that we are positioned well for it to happen at any time. We understand that the horrors being played out everywhere are things that were predicted, prophesied in His Word.

We have so much going on right now. Social issues that 40 years ago would not have been discussed, the worldwide economy failing and now the threat of another military action and possibly war. If you listen to the media and many of our government officials, it is easy to slip into a state of fear.

Some of this, I believe, is planned by those in power because people who are in fear lean more on the government and that is what they want. As a matter of fact, if the fear is too strong, the people will clamor for the government to be even more involved. They will be will be willing to give up more of their freedoms to have the government entangle them with more controls, in the name of eliminating fear.

Much of it is hyperbole. However, some of the information we get are real and speaks of the danger. Danger to our freedoms, family life, finances, health and welfare. These purveyors of truth bring solid information to those who will listen. Godly men and women who have taken on the mantle of keeping us informed.

We need to double our efforts and dig in, staying prayed up. Trouble is all around us, but this is exactly why we are going to go verse by verse through this chapter of protection. It will help to equip us not only as individuals, but also help us to be able to cover our families, friends and companies adequately in this protection. Once done I will supply you with a confession that you can print out and use daily, one that is personalized.

This verse sets the stage for our safety, and reiterates the idea of digging in. Two words "dwell" and "abide" have some of the same definitions with slight nuances. Dwell means to sit in ambush, as a judge or in quiet; to remain, to marry, to inhabit, to keep house.

He that returns, he that marries, he that keeps house with God will remain under the defense of the Almighty. God doesn't want us to drop by only occasionally just to say "Hello" and then come running home when we are in trouble or danger.

What I see as our largest obstacle in having this relationship, our choosing to dwell with God, is a false fear. We fear that God will ask more of us than we are willing to give. There is such an element of the unknown in getting involved with God, and many of our churches make it seem so much like a spooky or uncommon thing.

We often relate the relationship with the Almighty God and his Kingdom with what we see on television and at the theaters. Hollywood has done a grave disservice to humanity in promoting the evil aspects of the supernatural. The problem is that they are promoting the B-Team, the team that should be sitting time out on the bench, the team that always loses in the end.

They don't tell the story about the insidious nature of evil, instead make it high level action film that is meant to titillate the senses and scare the daylights out of folks.

Where most of us are fooled, deceived, tricked into wrong doing through wrong thinking, they are showing evil as being snatched out of your bed, dragged into the darkness.

Instead of looking at the true opposite of what moviegoers see on the screen and becoming excited by the picture of love near indescribable, being provided for beyond their imagination, living a life of goodness and strength....folks take away the spooky and frightening element of the supernatural and think that we may be dragged screaming into the night by God.

The inference is that he is the same kind of a taskmaster as the devilish creatures depicted in the films. People use these big dollar productions as a standard by which they measure God and his A-Team.

God and his Kingdom is less spooky than I had ever imagined. He wants our relationship with Him to be as if we were married. Being married is a voluntary intimate union between man and woman.

When you are intimate with someone you know them very well and like them very much; it is private and friendly and makes you feel relaxed and comfortable; it is having someone to whom private matters are confided; you and this person have mutual interests or affections; you have an established friendship, which fosters a warm or friendly atmosphere; especially through smallness and informality (like an intimate gathering).

It does take time to develop this relationship, I'm not going to lie to you about that. But if you had a charismatic person come into your life, someone you were drawn to inexplicably, wouldn't you make the time to get to know that person? Wouldn't you take this person's phone calls, texts and emails? If they were on television, wouldn't you take the time to watch that show and cheer them on? Would you choose to eat dinner with them or celebrate a holiday with them?

Well, what happens if an additional person comes into your life with different qualities but the same draw? Would you say, "I have no more room in my life?" Would you turn down a marriage proposal from Mr. or Ms. Right because you had no room for this intimate relationship? Unfortunately, many do.

This is what even proclaiming Christians do daily. They for some reason don't seem to desire and are even afraid to have this relationship where they get to know Him as well as He knows them. And yet, they have relationships with mere men, who are severely lacking.

Let me say, this relationship is anything but spooky. It is more real than many flesh and blood relationships that I have had. It is a very private and friendly relationship, I feel God's love. I am no longer skittish around Him. Instead, I am comfortable and relaxed. I talk to him about everything. He knows the worst of me and loves me through it.

He doesn't even bring up my past, except as a warning toward a future event that I can't see. Not only am I interested in the same things as He is, I have found that He is interested, truly interested in the things that I am. When we are together the atmosphere is warm and friendly and most of the time informal. I don't have to speak to him as if He is a far off official who carries the balance of my well-being in his hands (fear based).

Instead, I speak to Him as a child, coming to him without fear, full of expectation and knowing that He has power to provide for me and also given me the power to carry out my part in the world. It is a near indescribable relationship, but it is wonderful. And in the embrace of this relationship comes the protection spoken about here.

Your relationship doesn't have to be complete, we are all at different levels of relationship with God. So no matter where in this relationship you are, as long as you are in that hiding place, protection is yours. Now claim it for yourself.

Good morning, Father. Thank you for the offer of the relationship of a lifetime. Thank you for dispelling wrong thoughts about what this relationship means, erasing from our minds the hyperbole of the media, the government and Hollywood. Thank you for security we can find no other place and the peace that brings. Through our peaceful demeanor in the midst of crisis, people will be drawn to you. In Jesus' name, we praise and thank you....Amen!

Definitions used in today's study:
Dwelleth - a primitive root; properly **to *sit* down (specifically as judge, in ambush, in quiet)**; by implication to *dwell*, **to *remain***; causative **to *settle*, to *marry*** :- (make to) abide (-ing), continue, (cause to, make to) dwell (-ing), ease self, endure, establish, × fail, habitation, haunt, (make to) **inhabit** (-ant), make to keep [house], lurking, × marry (-ing), (bring again to) place, remain, return, seat, set (-tle), (down-) sit (-down, still, -ting down, -ting [place] -uate), take, **tarry**.
Secret - or (feminine) cithrah, sith-raw'; (Deut. 32:38), from <H5641> (cathar); **a cover** (in a good or a bad, a literal or a figurative sense) :- backbiting, covering, covert, × disguise [-th],

hiding place, **privily [confidentially or in secret]**, **protection**, secret (-ly, place); a primitive root; to hide (by covering), literal or figurative :- be absent, keep close, **conceal**, hide (self), (keep) secret, × surely.

High - from <H5927> (`alah); an elevation, i.e. (adjective) lofty (comparative); as title, **the Supreme** :- (Most, on) high (-er, -est), upper (-most); a primitive root; to ascend, intransitive (be high) or active (mount); used in a great variety of senses, primary and secondary, literal and figurative (as follow) :- arise (up), (cause to) **ascend up**, at once, break [the day] (up), bring (up), (cause to) burn, carry up, cast up, + shew, climb (up), (cause to, make to) come (up), cut off, dawn, depart, exalt, excel, fall, fetch up, get up, (make to) go (away, up), grow (over), **increase**, lay, leap, levy, lift (self) up, light, [make] up, × mention, mount up, offer, make to pay, + **perfect**, **prefer**, put (on), **raise**, **recover**, **restore**, (make to) rise (up), scale, set (up), shoot forth (up), (begin to) spring (up), stir up, take away (up), work.

Abide - or liyn, leen; a primitive root; **to stop (usually over night)**; by implication **to stay permanently**; hence (in a bad sense) **to be obstinate (especially in words, to complain)** :- abide (all night), continue, **dwell**, **endure**, grudge, be left, lie all night, (cause to) lodge (all night, in, -ing, this night), (make to) murmur, **remain**, **tarry (all night, that night)**.

Shadow - from <H6751> (tsalal); **shade**, whether literal or figurative :- **defence**, shade (-ow); a primitive root [rather identical with <H6749> (tsalal) **through the idea of hovering over** (compare <H6754> (tselem))]; to shade, **as twilight or an opaque object** :- begin to be dark, shadowing; from an unused root meaning to shade; a phantom, i.e. (figurtive) illusion, **resemblance**; hence **a representative figure**, especially an idol :- **image**, vain shew.

Almighty - from <H7703> (shadad); the Almighty :- Almighty; a primitive root; properly **to be burly [muscular, strong, and heavy built]**, i.e. (figurative) **powerful (passive impregnable [well protected, unable to be taken by storm])**; by implication

to ravage :- dead, destroy (-er), oppress, robber, spoil (-er), ×
utterly, (lay) waste.

.

CHAPTER 2

Determining Strong Alliances

Psalm 91:2 (KJV)

2 I will say (underline: answer, avouch: take it to the bank, consider, declare, determine) of the LORD (self-Existent, Eternal, Jehovah, Yah'weh), He is my refuge (shelter, hope, to flee for protection, confide in, put trust in) and my fortress (a net, castle, defense, strong place, bulwark, besieging tower, munitions: defensive structure, weapons, hunt, take provision, lunch especially for a journey) : my God (gods in the ordinary sense, but specifically used of the supreme God); in him will I trust (to hie [step on it] for refuge], be confident or sure, careless; marked by lack of attention or consideration or forethought or thoroughness).

This forceful statement of clarity can be said over our lives every day and in any precarious situation. It sounds like this:

-   I answer as of the LORD (the Most High God), any bad situation or dangerous circumstance

-   I avouch, and can take it to the bank….

-   I have considered, determined and declared the Lord is these things....

This declaration is of the Most Supreme Being caring for us to the extent that he protects us, no matter the degree of trouble we find ourselves in, is an amazing thought. If you choose to say this, even if you are full of fear at that moment, peace begins to flood your consciousness.

Courage makes you stand a little taller. You are no longer small and the problem big. Instead, you begin to see yourself protected and with every resource to answer the forces opposing you. The more you get the words of this chapter embedded in your mind and heart, the greater degree of that "peace that passes all understanding" you gain.

He is our Creator and our God, someone so close. He is someone in whom we can place our hope (earnest expectation), someone in whom we can confide our deepest fears, thoughts and desires. He is not only a person He is a place. A place of refuge, a shelter, and a place where you flee for protection.

The protection spoken of is described in words that paint a mental picture of a castle, its weapons and bulwarks made of some of the thickest and strongest materials. A bulwark is a protective structure of stone or concrete; extending from the shore into the water to prevent a beach from washing away. This can be carried over into the abstract and mean someone or something that protects or defends something such as a belief, idea, or a way of life. This picture was meant to give us the idea of an impenetrable defense.

These words are spoken over our lives initiating spiritual movement; it ignites the spiritual forces and sounds the alarm. When we run to His protection, we can expect that it is infallible and worry melts away. It is not only protection, but provision, as well. Until this moment, I had never seen that aspect of the word "fortress," but there it is.

Many of the words used to describe both the word itself and the root word "fortress" are hunting terms; net, snare, be hunted, catches, hunter. So the idea of provision or food ties into this line of thought. I have never seen this as a provision verse before this time, however.

The balance of the declaration states He is "my God." The word used here speaks of "gods in the ordinary sense, but specifically used of the supreme God." I was going to say, back in those days people had their choice of many gods, and so it is understandable that the person is making a specific declaration of this particular god, "my God." But our studies always attempt to find a thread to our current time and our day to day lives.

If we look at our life and times, we can see that there are believers in God, the triune being; the Father, Son and Holy Spirit. Some have believed in God but aren't convinced of Jesus and/or the Holy Spirit. There are, also, believers in darkness. Those who believe in no Supreme being, they basically believe in themselves or humanity as the supreme force.

There are those who believe in government as their god. We also have gods and images of all sorts, anything from food and alcohol, business and money to television and entertainment, to other people and, unfortunately, even ourselves.

So, we make choices about what we will believe in and whom we will align ourselves with, whether we have looked at it in this manner or not. Making a statement during a daily confession that "I say of the Lord, He is my refuge, protection, hope and my fortress, defense, and provision for the journey; my God" is a big deal.

It is a statement that telegraphs within our being and also in the material and spiritual world. It sounds a warning to enemies and call of unity to friends. It is a statement that builds confidence in God's desire to move in our behalf. This confidence isn't only seen within us but also, our allies. We begin to expect good and justice.

This statement also generates caution and fear in those who would attempt to come against us. This declaration is a statement of trust and confidence in His ability to protect and provide, spoken daily, adds another brick to that wall of confidence each time it is said. It is how confidence is built.

Good morning, Father. Thank you for this blueprint that with use, with daily confession, builds our human confidence in You, our supernatural and Almighty God. This is also a declaration that places you above all the other gods that are available and lessens their ability to snare our attention away from you. Thank you for how when these words are spoken initiate spiritual movement in our behalf, for the protection and provision this understanding provides. We open ourselves to developing our confidence during each day through meditation, pray and confession. Open our eyes to the needs of others and help us meet the needs of those we are assigned to. In Jesus' name, we praise and thank you....Amen!

Definitions used in today's study:

Say - a primitive root; to say (used with great latitude) :- **answer**, appoint, **avouch [take it to the bank]**, bid, boast self, call, certify, challenge, charge, + (at the, give) command (-ment), commune, **consider**, **declare**, demand, × desire, **determine**, × expressly, × indeed, × intend, name, × plainly, promise, publish, report, require, say, speak (against, of), × still, × suppose, talk, tell, term, × that is, × think, use [speech], utter, × verily, × yet.

Lord - from <H1961> (hayah); (the) self-Existent or Eternal; Jehovah, Jewish national name of God :- Jehovah, the Lord. Compare <H3050> (Yahh), <H3069> (Yehovih); a primitive root [compare <H1933> (hava')]; to exist, i.e. be or become, come to pass (always emphatic, and not a mere copula or auxiliary) :- beacon, × altogether, be (-come, accomplished, committed, like), break, cause, come (to pass), do, faint, fall, + follow, happen, × have, last, pertain, quit (one-) self, require, × use.

Refuge - or machceh, makh-seh'; from <H2620> (chacah); **a shelter** (literal or figurative) :- **hope**, (place of) refuge, shelter, trust; a primitive root; **to flee for protection** [compare <H982> (batach)]; figurative **to confide in** :- have hope, make refuge, **(put) trust**.

Fortress - or (feminine) metsuwdah, mets-oo-daw'; or metsudah, mets-oo-daw'; for <H4685> (matsowd); **a net**, or (abstract) capture; also a fastness :- **castle**, **defence**, fort (-ress), (strong) hold, be hunted, net, snare, **strong place**; or (feminine) metsowdah, mets-o-daw'; or metsodah, mets-o-daw'; from <H6679> (tsuwd); a net (for capturing animals or fishes); also (by interch. for <H4679> (metsad)) a fastness or (besieging) tower :- **bulwark**, hold, munition, net, snare; a primitive root; to lie alongside (i.e. in wait); by implication to catch an animal (figurative men); (denominative from <H6718> (tsayid)) to victual (for a journey) :- chase, **hunt**, sore, **take (provision)**; from a form of <H6679> (tsuwd) and meaning the same; the chase; also game (thus taken); (general) **lunch (especially for a journey)** :- × catcheth, food, × hunter, (that which he took in) hunting, venison, victuals.

God - plural of <H433> ('elowahh); **gods in the ordinary sense; but specifically used (in the plural thus, especially with the article) of the supreme God**; occasionally applied by way of deference to magistrates; and sometimes as a superlative :- angels, × exceeding, God (gods) (-dess, -ly), × (very) great, judges, × mighty; rarely (shortened) 'eloahh, el-o'-ah; probably prolonged (emphatic) from <H410> ('el); a deity or the Deity :- God, god. See <H430> ('elohiym); shortened from <H352> ('ayil); strength; as adjective mighty; especially the Almighty (but used also of any deity) :- God (god), × goodly, × great, idol, might (-y one), power, strong. Compare names in "-el."

Trust - a primitive root; properly **to hie [step on it] for refuge** [but not so precipatately as <H2620> (chacah)]; figurative to trust, be confident or sure :- be bold (confident, secure, sure), **careless [effortless and unstudied, marked by lack of attention or consideration or forethought or thoroughness]** (one, woman), put confidence, (make to) hope, (put, make to) trust.

CHAPTER 3

Defense Without Fail

Psalm 91:3 (KJV)

3 Surely he shall deliver (<u>snatch away, defend, deliver, without fail, preserve, recover, rescue, save</u>) thee from the snare (<u>a spring net, a sheet, to batter out</u>) of the fowler (<u>entangled, someone who hunts wild bird for food</u>), and from the noisome (<u>eagerly coveting and rushing upon, desire, calamity, perverse thing, naughty, mischief, iniquity, wickedness; to breathe, to be</u>) pestilence (<u>a pernicious evil influence, serious disease that spreads fast and kills many, plague, to arrange, to speak, to subdue, work, promise</u>).

What does the word deliver mean to us. When we are delivered, we are brought to the destination. As a package, sent through many of our fine carrier services throughout the world. I say this with a bit of a smile on my face, because I see at least one of our number cringing at the idea that these services are "fine." A couple of bad experiences with one of these might make a person a bit leery of this promise.

But in this example we are talking about a person or company that is fallible, not about God, who has no flaw in Him. When we are delivered, we are free from harm or evil. When we are delivered, we have brought into existence through birth.

This verse talks to us about all the things which he will bring us out. A fowler is a person who hunts wild birds for food. There is no inherent evil in a fowler, but the text uses this analogy to describe the way God's enemy (and ours) goes about pulling us away from our original destination. Stop and think about it.

One of the definitions of deliver is to bring to a destination. We know that it is the enemy's job; his goal to kill, steal and destroy. He delights in killing our dreams, stealing our ambition through berating us and disappointment, and destroying not only the physical body but our hearts, our passion.

It makes him just as happy to have us walking around asleep or operating in resignation, in life. He gets a kick out of us believing that living a mediocre life is more than most can really expect, I mean, at least we aren't living on the street...right?

God says that He will surely deliver us from all of these mindsets and ungodly circumstances. However, our enemy wants us to believe and get us ensnared, trapped into mindsets where we think that it is not only necessary but normal to:

-    Covet what others have, rushing in on them and taking what we want...after all if we don't look out for ourselves who will

- Live in a constant flux of calamity and that suffering and that loss is a normal way of life

- Create mischief (causing trouble, not always serious harm) in our own lives and the lives of others around us, that it is humorous

- See and tolerate behavior in not only our children but adults who should know better as normal and right

- Condone perverse behavior in our own life and the circle in which we move. Perverseness can be immoral behavior, but also a general oppositional attitude; consistently being contrary.

- See wrong and call it right out of a desire to be politically correct

- Grow old before our time and move backward instead of living life to the full and moving forward

The goal is to subdue us from any good and fruitful activity. We continue to see in the definitions of the words we study filled with references to abundance, plenty and prosperity. The enemy wants us to believe that this bounty is just for a chosen few rather than every person who reads them.

What have we seen? God's promises include audacious supply of all good things. We have the ability to have a heart peace that passes all understanding. This relationship gives us the ability to live without financial debt. We learn that we have the ability to live out the dreams that God placed in our hearts. We begin to understand our worth to God and society. We know we have the ability to influence others positively with our actions and words. We find that amazing protection is supplied to us within these words.

All of these things are sanctioned by the Almighty God for our lives. He is not trying to keep us from these things, but instead, deliver us to these promised destination points.

Good morning, Father. Thank you for peace, a peace that passes all understanding. These words don't say we won't have negative things come against us, but that when they do that you are there snatching us away from the trouble facing us. It is your choice to confound the enemy and laugh at him, and we can enjoy this, as well. Thank you for these word studies as they open our minds to greater depths of the words and expand our understanding of the meaning of the promise. Although we may never know the complete fullness of it, and we know that each of us will focus on one point, or another within a particular verse depending on our own personal current events, we all will grow each time we read these words. We open ourselves to know and understand more. When we do, our wisdom expands and in this; we are more able to help those who cross our paths. In Jesus' name, we praise and thank you....Amen!

Definitions used in today's study:
Deliver - a primitive root; **to snatch away**, whether in a good or a bad sense :- × at all, **defend**, deliver (self), escape, × **without fail**, part, **pluck**, **preserve**, **recover**, **rescue**, rid, **save**, spoil, strip, × surely, take (out).
Snare - from <H6351> (pachach); **a (metallic) sheet (as pounded thin)**; also **a spring net** (as spread out like a lamina) :- gin, (thin) plate, snare; a primitive root; to batter out; but used

only as denominative from <H6341> (pach), to spread a net :- be snared

Fowler - passive participle of <H3369> (yaqosh); properly **entangled**, i.e. by implication (intransitive) **a snare**, or (transitive) a snarer :- fowler, snare; a primitive root; to ensnare (literal or figurative) :- fowler (lay a) snare.

Noisome - from <H1933> (hava') (**in the sense of eagerly coveting and rushing upon**; **by implication of falling**); **desire**; also ruin :- **calamity**, iniquity, mischief, mischievous (thing), naughtiness, naughty, noisome, **perverse thing**, substance, very **wickedness**; or havah, haw-vaw'; a primitive root [compare <H183> ('avah), <H1961> (hayah)] supposed to mean properly **to breathe; to be (in the sense of existence)** :- be, × have.

Pestilence - from <H1696> (dabar) (in the sense of destroying); a pestilence :- murrain, **pestilence [a pernicious evil influence, a serious disease that spreads fast and kills many people]**, **plague [any serious disease that spreads quickly to a lot of people and usually ends in death]**; a primitive root; perhaps **properly to arrange**; but used **figuratively (of words) to speak**; **rarely (in a destructive sense) to subdue** :- answer, appoint, bid, command, commune, declare, destroy, give, name, promise, pronounce, rehearse, say, speak, be spokesman, subdue, talk, teach, tell, think, use [entreaties], utter, × well, × work.

CHAPTER 4

Hedge, Feathers & Thorns, You're Covered

Psalm 91:4 (KJV)

4 He shall cover (<u>to fence in, protect, hedge in</u>) thee with his feathers (<u>wing, feather, pinion [larger feather]</u>), and under his wings (<u>an edge or extremity, a flap, overspreading</u>) shalt thou trust (<u>flee for protection, confide in, have hope, make refuge</u>): his truth (<u>stability, certainty, establishment, faithful, to build support, nurture as parent</u>) shall be thy shield (<u>a hook, large shield, be prickly like thorn</u>) and buckler (<u>something surrounding the person</u>).

The role of a parent or nurse is to foster growth and development in their charges, their children. Children grow to trust the person who becomes established as their primary caregiver. The closest bond is developed between the child and this person as they spend valuable time together.

If the caregiver has a close bond with the Almighty, the understanding of this holy bond is transferred to the child. And when this understanding is passed to the child, his confidence in the desire and competence of God as Father and protector of their life increases, and does so early in life.

This is not the way that many of us have grown up, but instead have had to learn of the Father's willingness and desire to care for us later in life. This is not always an easy task because we have years of prior programming and experiences to contend. Programming and experience that doesn't seem to support the claims we read in the Bible.

We read these words, and they inspire hope. But at first glance and often through deep searching, we can't see evidence of this being the case to this point. God has provided repetition in His word of precepts, His character traits and His processes to break down years of past programming. The word carries life in it and with repeated reading and meditating, and speaking our hope and faith are ignited.

This is no condemnation of a particular generation of people. But instead, throughout all generations it has been more the norm than the exception to treat God as someone far off that we need to beg and plead for assistance in hard times, and choose to keep Him at a distance the rest of the time. I believe this is done because of a lack of understanding the immense love he has for us.

We have been taught whether in the church or outside that He is a hard taskmaster, rather than a loving parent who desires and is willing and able to help us improve in life and become more successful. As with all parents, the issue of safety is paramount.

What parent would allow injury to come to their children without going to war for them? The moment they become aware of danger coming in the path of their charge, they run between that danger and child producing a cover. With each show of protection, or rescue from a storm, or show of keeping out an enemy by surrounding us with a prickly hedge our confidence in His stable standing towards us grows.

The transition begins when we keep His word handy and give voice to those words when we are facing circumstances that threaten us. We ease ourselves from fear to faith without making any other move than choosing to speak these words of protection. It is a supernatural act when we speak, amazing in its power and force.

Whether we have come to the party early or late, our confidence in God can and will deepen with each positive experience in our relationship with Him. If you notice I continue to speak about relationship, this is because it is a common theme in God's word. The more we show our desire to relationship, the more we see Him moving in our behalf and, the more engrained our faith.

These right words spoken over your life are far more powerful than any physical move of self-protection you could ever attempt.

Good morning, Father. Thank you for the hedge around us and the overspreading of your wings in our lives. We have often heard of the protection you afford us like that of a big strong brother behind us (depicted as the smaller and weaker one)....that when an enemy comes attempting to bully us they are faced with your figure behind us. And Father, that this brawny figure behind us frightens off the meanest and ugliest of attackers. Even though it is wholly inadequate, we are grateful for this picture. When we speak these words over our life, we initiate a chain of events in the spiritual realm and our faith in Your willingness to protect us and in the process itself grows. When I think of your wrath turned upon those who want to hurt us in any way, who choose to toy with our emotions, who deceive us into wrong decision-making....well, I near feel sorry for that person that was used by the spirit behind the unkind act. I am grateful to know that your wrath is reserved for those forces outside the family and that, for us, your correction is always guided by love and a desire to see us grow past the offense. We open ourselves for a deeper confidence in your desire to keep us safe. Help us in these last days to show the same love to the people you place in our path and our charge. And Lord, we pray for Israel and the peace of Jerusalem. We pray wisdom in the decision making that is going on in our government in these next few days. We ask for a Bible based, God response....one that will support allies properly and consider our countries safety, as well as the safety of the world. In Jesus' name, we praise and thank you....Amen!

Definitions used in today's study:
Cover - or sakak, saw-kak'; (Exod. 33:22), a primitive root; properly **to entwine as a screen**; by implication **to fence in**, cover over, (figurative) **protect** :- cover, **defence**, defend, **hedge in**, join together, set, shut up.
Feathers - feminine of <H83> ('eber) :- **feather, wing**; from <H82> ('abar); a pinion :- [long-] wing (-ed); a primitive root; **to soar** :- fly.
Wings - from <H3670> (kanaph); **an edge or extremity**; specifically (of a bird or army) a wing, (**of a garment or bed-clothing**) **a flap**, (of the earth) a quarter, (of a building) a pinnacle :- + bird, border, corner, end, feather [-ed], × flying, +

(one an-) other, overspreading, × quarters, skirt, × sort, uttermost part, wing ([-ed]); a primitive root; properly to project laterally, i.e. probably (reflexive) to withdraw :- be removed.

Trust - a primitive root; **to flee for protection** [compare <H982> (batach)]; figurative **to confide in** :- **have hope**, **make refuge**, (put) trust.

Truth - contraction from <H539> ('aman); **stability**; figurative **certainty**, truth, trustworthiness :- assured (-ly), **establishment**, **faithful**, right, sure, true (-ly, -th), verity; a primitive root; properly **to build up or support**; **to foster as a parent or nurse**; figurative **to render (or be) firm or faithful**, to trust or believe, **to be permanent or quiet**; moral to be true or certain; once (Isa. 30:21; by interchange for <H541> ('aman)) to go to the right hand :- hence assurance, believe, bring up, establish, + fail, be faithful (of long continuance, stedfast, sure, surely, trusty, verified), nurse, (-ing father), (put), trust, turn to the right.

Shield - feminine of <H6791> (tsen); **a hook (as pointed)**; also **a (large) shield (as if guarding by prickliness)**; also cold (as piercing) :- buckler, cold, hook, shield, target; from an unused root meaning **to be prickly**; **a thorn**; hence a cactus-hedge :- thorn.

Buckler - properly active participle feminine of <H5503> (cachar); **something surrounding the person**, i.e. a shield :- buckler; a primitive root; to travel round (specifically as a pedlar); intensive to palpitate :- go about, merchant (-man), occupy with, pant, trade, traffick.

CHAPTER 5

Succumbing to Fear Idolizes the Enemy

Psalm 91:5 (KJV)

5 Thou shalt not be afraid (to fear, to revere, dread or worry) for the terror (sudden alarm, the feeling of fear, be startled, fear in general, stand in awe) by night (a twist away from light, adversity, to fold back); nor for the arrow (piercer, wound, of God a thunder-bolt, to sever, be curtailed-reduce, limit, restrict, terminate or abbreviate before intended time) that flieth (covered, obscured-not known well, not understood or less visible/unclear, brandish-waving about or exhibit aggressively) by day (daily, to by hot, daylight hours, full day-one sunset to another, perpetually, in trouble);

We have a loving Father who has gained our confidence in some degree. Not only has he proven his willingness to protect us, but we have seen and experienced the benefit of his protective actions. With each new experience and with each new confession of His protection we gain in faith that it will happen for us the next time, as well.

Yesterday we discussed the fact that faith or confidence is not always exercised by us. We have to train ourselves in recognizing fear and put together an arsenal of tools we can use to stand firm. Early on we need to step out in a blind faith.

It is not that as born-again Christians that have not been given this measure of faith, but when not exercised that muscle is not as ready for a fight. A combination of wanting to change our condition in life, study, choosing to meditate continually on and hear the word, speaking the word and having a network of people who can stand with us in difficult times helps to build and maintain faith.

Even when faith is great, we will continue to have situations come against us.

If we look at the word translated as day, it can mean time frames of daylight hours or full 24 hour periods. However, the first definition is "daily." One of the definitions of the root word for "day" is "perpetually." If we take these definitions at face value, we will have to concede that troubles of all sorts are going to be a part of our future.

Trouble will be knocking at our door on a daily basis. It is our choice whether we will let it in or not. Even when it does come, these verses tell us that we have no reason to fear. These are not the only verses that speak of this supernatural protection. Confirmation of this theme runs throughout the Book.

Now let's take a look at the word translated as afraid. "Thou shall not be afraid;" thou shall not fear, because when we do show fear and respond in fear it is showing reverence to Satan and his forces. We are by the definitions of this word confronted with an implied caution.

The caution is to focus our reverence on our God, not the enemy forces.

Revere means:

-    to have a lot of respect and admiration for someone or something

-    regard with feelings of respect and reverence

-    consider hallowed or exalted or be in awe of

-    love unquestioningly and uncritically or to excess

-    to venerate as an idol (venerate: to respect or worship someone or something, regard with feelings of respect and reverence; consider hallowed or exalted or be in awe of)

We don't always consider this negative affect of our succumbing to fear. However, if we allow ourselves to be overwhelmed by fear, we are essentially bowing a knee to our enemy rather than running to our Father for the protection he has liberally promised us.

Now that we understand more clearly how we show our alliance when we fear, exactly what types of feelings and actions does fear encumber?

Fear can mean; worry (nervous and upset feelings about a problem or the outcome of a problem, anxiety), a sudden alarm (fear from the awareness of danger), it can be a generalized or gnawing feeling….nothing particular to be afraid of, but something is there. The arrow spoken of here not only means some sharp instrument that can cause physical wounds, but also mean something curtails us.

Curtailing is anything that restricts our thinking our speaking and our actions. It means to terminate something before it reached its desired goal or before its time was complete. It means to reduce or limit. As all of the definitions of fear and terror speak specifically of the non-physical and thinking realm, the definitions pertaining to "arrow" could mean either physical or spiritual or emotional curtailment.

These feelings can be generated by adversity and are made worse when we bend to fear when it comes knocking. Bending, twisting away from the light (God's Light) or folding back is in essence a spiritual flinch. When a flinch is seen by an adversary, they feel emboldened to move forward with their attack.

When we flinch, we instinctively feel less prepared to stand our ground, feel weaker. We feel as if in flinching we have signaled our weakness to the enemy in front of us. These are some of the words used to define the night in which that fear appears.

The night spoken of, has more to do with our potential reaction to fear and the day speaks more to how the weapons of the enemy come at us. Specifically, they come either by an aggressive exhibit and assault, or they come, hidden from view, obscured from sight. To me these two ways to come at us are the extremes at either end of the spectrum?

One attack would come at us as if in a shoot-out at the OK Corral, guns blazing. The other attack would be a sneaky assault, as someone putting small amounts of poison in your food over a long period of time. Death would be the outcome of both if you weren't properly protected.

Everything in between these two extremes is also on the table. And I have to say, from my experience, the enemy hasn't failed to use any and every weapon or assault mode against me and my family. Nothing has been off limits, anything that will work; he will use. This is where our response comes into play.

We have the option to allow fear in all its forms to run roughshod over our lives, or stop it dead in its tracks. We have far more power over our thoughts and feelings than many think. I used to be one of those people who were a slave to my feelings. Fear and worry dominated my life. It took time to change that.

Why? First of all being controlled by feelings, fear and worry is a habit we learn. The earlier we are programmed with this style of negative thinking, the more diligent we need to be in standing against it. If this is a problem area for you, you need to admit to it before you can address it.

Then we need to understand that this is not the way God desires us to live. His plan for our victorious life includes being strong in all aspects; physically, emotionally, mentally and spiritually. Now that we have this awareness, we seek out the verses within the Bible on which to stand firmly.

And then, when a contrary thought, a worried thought or fear-filled thought comes and we begin to crumble; we choose to pull out these verses and rehearse them verbally. Yes, I mean, out loud. An amazing change begins the moment you do.

Good morning, Father. Thank you for showing us this information about how fear affects us and the 'news' to some of us that walking around in fear or worry is showing an alliance with the enemy rather than you. It is a harsh pill to swallow, but one we need to be made aware of. It is important for us to understand what can be lost by opening the door to and entertaining fear. We choose instead to accept and stand firmly in your protection, we choose to nurture heart peace and joy. We open ourselves to your direction in gathering the tools and learning about the weapons of our warfare....knowing that they never fail us. As we become more and more comfortable in this protected state, we will be better able to help others in our circle who also struggle with fear. We live in a world where there is plenty to be concerned about if we don't know you, help us to be a stabilizing force within the circles we move. We pray Father for the peace of Jerusalem....the protection of Israel. In Jesus' holy name, we praise and thank you....Amen!

Definitions used in today's study:
Afraid - a primitive root; **to fear**; moral **to revere**; causative **to frighten** :- affright, **be (make) afraid**, **dread** (-ful), (put in) fear (-ful, -fully, -ing), (be had in) reverence (-end), × see, terrible (act, -ness, thing).
Terror - from <H6342> (pachad); **a (sudden) alarm** (properly **the object feared**, by implication **the feeling**) :- dread (-ful), fear, (thing) great [fear, -ly feared], terror; a primitive root; **to be startled** (by a sudden alarm); hence **to fear in general** :- be afraid, **stand in awe**, (be in) fear, make to shake.
Night - or (Isa. 21:11) leyl, lale; also layelah, lah'-yel-aw; from the same as <H3883> (luwl); properly **a twist (away of the light)**, i.e. night; figurative **adversity** :- ([mid-]) night (season); from an unused root meaning **to fold back**; **a spiral step** :- **winding stair**. Compare <H3924> (lula'ah).

Arrow - from <H2686> (chatsats); properly **a piercer**, i.e. an arrow; by implication **a wound**; figurative **(of God) thunderbolt**; (by interchange for <H6086> (`ets)) **the shaft of a spe**ar :- + archer, arrow, dart, shaft, staff, wound; a primitive root [compare <H2673> (chatsah)]; properly **to chop into**, **pierce or sever**; hence **to curtail [reduce, limit, restrict, terminate or abbreviate before its intended]**, **to distribute (into ranks)**; as denominative from <H2671> (chets), to shoot an arrow :- archer, × bands, cut off in the midst.

Flieth - a primitive root; **to cover (with wings or obscurity);** hence (as denominative from <H5775> (`owph)) to fly; also (by implication of dimness) **to faint (from the darkness of swooning)** :- **brandish [the act of waving exhibit aggressively]**, be **(wax) faint**, flee away, fly (away), × set, shine forth, weary; from <H5774> (`uwph); a bird (as covered with feathers, or rather as covering with wings), often collective :- bird, that flieth, flying, fowl.

Day - from <H3117> (yowm); **daily** :- daily, (by, in the) day (-time); from an unused root meaning **to be hot**; a day (as the warm hours), whether literal (**from sunrise to sunset, or from one sunset to the next**), or figurative (a space of time defined by an associated term), [often used adverbially] :- age, + always, + chronicles, continually (-ance), daily, ([birth-], each, to) day, (now a, two) days (agone), + elder, × end, + evening, + (for) ever (-lasting, -more), × full, life, as (so) long as (...live), (even) now, + old, + outlived, + **perpetually**, presently, + remaineth, × required, season, × since, space, then, (process of) time, + as at other times, + **in trouble**, weather, (as) when, (a, the, within a) while (that), × whole (+ age), (full) year (-ly), + younger.

CHAPTER 6

Don't Be Afraid, You Have a Choice

Psalm 91:6 (KJV)

6 Nor for the pestilence (a pernicious evil influence, serious disease that spreads fast and kills many, plague, to arrange, to speak, to subdue, work, promise)that walketh (behave, conversant, exercise) in darkness (obscurity- not known well, not understood or less visible/unclear, privily- confidentially or secretly, set as the sun); nor for the destruction (to cut off, damage so severely that something stops existing or cannot be restored to its former state) that wasteth (to swell up, by implication of insolence-offensive disrespectful impudent acts, rudeness, impertinent, inclined to take liberties, to overwhelm, overpower or destroy) at noonday (dual double light).

Today's verse is an expansion of what not to fear, or as we learned yesterday bend our knee to. Pestilence can mean a physical disease or illness. When attacked in our physical body, by either illness or physical assault, our body hollers at us. The attack could happen through a person or accident, or we could experience a physical ailment.

No matter how it comes, our attention is being divided by the clamor of physical distress and believing for healing made manifest.

It is yelling at us for attention. It is crying out for us to spend our time and resources in an attempt to repair all that is broken there. All of a sudden, our situation is not something only in the physical realm, it is a situation that is also eating up our mental, emotional and financial resources. It chips away at our spiritual reserve.

Another definition of pestilence is pernicious evil influence. Pernicious means very dangerous or harmful, especially to someone's moral character, or working or spreading in a hidden and usually injurious way, or exceedingly harmful. In looking at the other ways pernicious can be used; perniciously; perniciousness we see these definitions, grave harmfulness, or deadliness. Noxiously baneful. Harmfully insidious manner.

Insidious means it is dangerous because it seems to be harmless or not important, but, in fact, it causes harm or damage; it was intended to entrap, to beguile but harmful, working in a spreading or hidden and injurious way. Noxious means poisonous, or injurious in either a physical or mental health. Baneful, deadly, sinister, or a foreshadow of evil or tragic developments, dishonorable.

These are the tools of the enemy. It is a repetition of yesterday's verse. Our enemies come at us in every conceivable manner. Physical, mental, emotional and spiritual. Evil comes through sneaking around, often dressed up as something harmless and beautiful but has within it poison that can take us down. But it also can come out in full force in the full light of day, guns blazing.

Brazen, rude, taking every liberty and meant to overwhelm, overpower and destroy.

The attacks come in every shape and size, but our answer is always God sized. Our defenses and our response are not physical or emotional. Instead our weapons are spoken of here:

2 Corinthians 10:4-6 (KJV)
4 (For the weapons of our warfare are not carnal, but mighty through God to the pulling down of strong holds;)
5 Casting down imaginations, and every high thing that exalteth itself against the knowledge of God, and bringing into captivity every thought to the obedience of Christ;
6 And having in a readiness to revenge all disobedience (inattention), when your obedience (attentive hearkening) is fulfilled.

These well-known verses tell us we have responsibility in this. We look at what comes to us from the outside world, we measure it against God's precepts, and within a moment we make a decision whether to accept this circumstance or not. We have the ability to counter all attacks with our thought process and the words we speak after the attack.

We either confirm or deny this circumstance right to stay as part of our life through our words.

It doesn't matter what form an attack takes. Our discernment comes through knowing the Word (study) and nudging by the Holy Spirit. The Holy Spirit is powerful, part of the Triune being. He knows every precept. He knows every word of the Bible. He knows every trick of the devil. Nurture your relationship with him and expect to receive his counsel in all situations.

Our responsibility is to compare constantly everything with what the Word says, however; it does not end there. We also need to speak God's words over our life as a protective cover against future attacks. If you have never read the Word or studied teachings by others, you can be sorely limited in your ability to respond.

It will be difficult to measure circumstances if you have no understanding of the Godly standard. It will be difficult to recognize the Holy Spirit's counsel, if you do not know his characteristics. The more you keep this Word in front of you, the harder it will be for you to be deceived, the harder for an attack to cause any real damage to you and your life.

Read the words of the Bible out loud not only during an attack, but as a covering before you are attacked. Covering your life with God given words is a preemptive strike against future attacks.

Good morning, Father. Thank you for a clearer understanding of the multitude of ways that we can be attacked....some subtle and some brazen, all meant to cause injury or cause death to us and/or our dreams. Thank you for our understanding why it is important to keep these words before our eyes and in our mouths. When we do so, they seep into our hearts. In the vault of our heart, they are kept as a shield that is ready for use to deflect the lying thieving ways of our enemy. Thank you for access to your Word that gives us an understanding of who you are and how you communicate with us, what you desire for us to have not only in the sweet by and by, but in this earth. We open ourselves to receive every blessing. In this blessed state, we are more able to move in the behalf of others. It is our responsibility to each day heal the world in whatever way we are able. We pray today, this 12th anniversary of the attack on our Nation, for protection of our people, for consolation of the family and friends of the men and women who were lost that day. We remember those who were lost that day and in subsequent years, as this anniversary has become a targeted time used by our enemies to attempt to chip away at our resources way of life. We pray for our Jewish friends, the peace of Jerusalem and Israel. We submit ourselves to you. In Jesus' name, we praise and thank you....Amen!

Definitions used in today's study:
Pestilence - from <H1696> (dabar) (in the sense of destroying); a pestilence :- murrain, **pestilence [a pernicious evil influence, a serious disease that spreads fast and kills many people], plague [any serious disease that spreads quickly to a lot of people and usually ends in death]**; a primitive root; perhaps **properly to arrange**; but used **figuratively (of words) to speak**; **rarely (in a destructive sense) to subdue** :- answer, appoint, bid, command, commune, declare, destroy, give, name, promise, pronounce, rehearse, say, speak, be spokesman, subdue, talk, teach, tell, think, use [entreaties], utter, × well, × work.
Walketh - akin to <H3212> (yalak); a primitive root; **to walk** (in a great variety of applications, literal and figurative) :- (all) along, apace, **behave (self)**, come, (on) continually, **be conversant**, depart, + be eased, enter, **exercise (self)**, + follow, forth, forward, get, go (about, abroad, along, away, forward, on, out, up and down), + greater, grow, be wont to haunt, lead, march, × more and more, move (self), needs, on, pass (away), be at the point, quite, run (along), + send, speedily, spread, still, surely, + tale-bearer, + travel (-ler), walk (abroad, on, to and fro, up and down, to places), wander, **wax**, [way-] faring man, × be weak, whirl; a primitive root [compare <H1980> (halak)]; to walk (literal or figurative); causative to carry (in various senses)

53

:- × again, away, bear, bring, carry (away), come (away), depart, flow, + follow (-ing), get (away, hence, him), (cause to, make) go (away, -ing, -ne, one's way, out), grow, lead (forth), let down, march, prosper, + pursue, cause to run, spread, take away ([-journey]), vanish, (cause to) walk (-ing), wax, × be weak.

Darkness - from the same as <H651> ('aphel); dusk :- darkness, **obscurity, privily [confidentially or secretly]**; from an unused root meaning to set as the sun; dusky :- very dark.

Destruction - from an unused root meaning **to cut off**; ruin :- destroying, **destruction [damage that is so severe that something stops existing or can never return to its normal state]**.

Wasteth - a primitive root; properly **to swell up**, i.e. figurative (**by implication of insolence [offensive disrespectful impudent act, the trait of being rude and impertinent; inclined to take liberties]**), **to devastate [overwhelm, overpower or destroy]** :- waste.

Noonday - from <H6671> (tsahar); a light (i.e. window); **dual double light**, i.e. noon :- midday, noon (-day, -tide), window; a primitive root; to glisten; used only as denominative from <H3323> (yitshar), to press out oil :- make oil.

CHAPTER 7

One in Ten Thousand

Psalm 91:7 (KJV)

7 A thousand shall fall at thy side, and ten thousand (<u>multiplied myriad</u>) at thy right hand (<u>the stronger more dexterous one</u>); but it shall not come nigh (<u>near, to attack, to give evidence for an argument, approach</u>) thee.

I'd like you to use your imagination to see the destruction that would have to occur for you to be in a situation (perhaps a battle, or maybe an earthquake) when there is a moment of silence as the roar of activity around you has stopped. You have just done your human best to cover yourself from the mayhem. The calamity had come so quickly that there was no time for you to pray about it.

In this eerie silence, you come out of hiding, and your first glimpse is what seems to be a thousand people lying dead. You are stunned, but as you begin to check your body for scrapes, bruises or broken bones, your eyes scan the area and realize that it is not only the thousand you originally thought. No, instead there is a number you can't count. The size of a medium sized town full of people has just been destroyed.

Now compare this with the public reaction when we have a tornado, and less than a hundred folks are lost. Or something more in the mind's eye because of the time of year, the devastation of the attack on the U.S. on September 11, 2001. In a city of over 8,000,000, three thousand people were lost. In both of these cases, people from around the country and world responded with prayer and contributions.

Looking at these numbers clinically, neither of the ratios of those who died vs. those who remained were close to the numbers seen in this verse. To my understanding, in my lifetime there has never been an occurrence where one person in ten-thousand or more was left alive after a calamity.

To make it clear to the mind's eye, a city the size of New York City would have out of 8,000,000 only 800 people left standing. That is an amazing claim being made by God in this verse. It is hard even to imagine those kinds of numbers. Most of us have a harder time imagining the depth of love and goodness that would keep us from the calamity, than being a victim of calamity.

Like it or not, we are programmed from birth to expect bad stuff to happen. We fight negative thoughts about whether we will have a job, or get a job, or get the prized promotion. We fight negative thoughts about how unfit we are for a relationship with Mr./Ms. Right, rather than looking at the good we have to offer.

We look at advertisement after advertisement about medications and assume it is normal to take anywhere from five to twenty-five different medications a day to be "healthy." Really? When did that happen? For every medication, you take there are a myriad of side-effects. You come up with another symptom. Instead of looking to see if that symptom is caused by the first med; they give you another tablet that causes more symptoms. Good gravy! It is an unholy mess out there.

God gave us a beautiful mind and wonderful promises. Let's begin to use them properly. The point in a statement like the one we find in this verse is meant to move us to using our imagination for the good rather than focusing on the bad. It is meant to change the focus of our mind from a Murphy's Law mentality to a God mentality.

If we see widespread flu in our country, rather than saying, "I get the flu every year, there is no way I will avoid this." Say, "If the flu is going around, it will just have to go around me. I haven't had the flu in years, and I don't intend on getting sick." This is the way to use our imagination in a productive and life giving way.

If you are up for a promotion begin saying, "If anyone is going to get this job, I will." Use your beautiful God given imagination, expecting God's hand to move for you, rather than identifying with your old thought processes stirred up by the enemy of your soul.

We need to realize that we have been easily defeated much of our lives by negativity that has hung over our lives as a cloud. We have not understood that we can discipline ourselves to live God inspired. Pick up the vision painted in this verse and begin to see how precious you are to the Almighty, and run with it.

Good morning, Father. Thank you for a love that elevates us above. This doesn't happen because we are better, it happens because we are beginning to see a secret of life. This secret tells us that this protection from major destruction can be very literal in wartime or natural disaster, but can be extended to the idea of your favor being so great in our lives that unless we succumb to negativity, we cannot fail with you in our camp. Thank you for helping us to change the image we have of you and your feelings for us. Thank you for a God image of what our future holds. It is not only our lives that are impacted negatively when we don't live life to our full potential, but multitudes are affected by it. It is imperative that we see life and our proper place in it, as you do. We pray for the peace of Jerusalem, the people of Israel. We ask to be used by you to see and serve those in our circle....and that with our technology this circle is enlarged. In Jesus' name, we praise and thank you....Amen!

Definitions used in today's study:

Thousand - properly the same as <H504> ('eleph); hence (an ox's head being the first letter of the alphabet, and this eventually used as a numeral) **a thousand** :- thousand; from <H502> ('alaph); a family; also (from the sense of yoking or taming) an ox or cow :- family, kine, oxen; a primitive root, to associate with; hence to learn (and causative to teach) :- learn, teach, utter.

Fall - a primitive root; **to _fall_,** in a great variety of applications (intransitive or causative, literal or figurative) :- be accepted, cast (down, self, [lots], out), **cease**, **die**, divide (by lot), **(let) fail**, (cause to, let, make, ready to) fall (away, down, -en, -ing), fell (-ing), fugitive, have [inheritance], inferior, be judged [_by mistake for_ <H6419> (palai)], lay (along), (cause to) lie down, light (down), be (× hast) lost, lying, overthrow, overwhelm, perish, present (-ed, -ing), **(make to) rot**, slay, smite out, × surely, throw down; a primitive root; to fall, in a great variety of applications (intransitive or causative, literal or figurative) :- be accepted, cast (down, self, [lots], out), cease, die, divide (by lot), (let) fail, (cause to, let, make, ready to) fall (away, down, -en, -ing), fell (-ing), fugitive, have [inheritance], inferior, be judged [by mistake for <H6419> (palai)], lay (along), (cause to) lie down, light (down), be (× hast) lost, lying, overthrow, overwhelm, perish, present (-ed, -ing), (make to) rot, slay, smite out, × surely, throw down.

Side - contracted from an unused root meaning to *sidle* off; **a *side***; figurative **an *adversary*** :- (be-) side.

Ten thousand - from <H7231> (rabab); **abundance** (in number), i.e. (specific) **a myriad** (whether defensive or indefensive) :- **many**, **million**, × multiply, ten thousand; a primitive root; properly **to cast together** [compare <H7241> (rabiyb)], i.e. increase, especially in number; also (as denominative from <H7233> (rebabah)) **to multiply by the myriad** :- increase, be many (-ifold), be more, multiply, **ten thousands**.

Right hand - from <H3231> (yaman); the right hand or side (leg, eye) of a person or other object (**as the stronger and more dexterous**); locally, the south :- + left-handed, right (hand, side), south; a primitive root; to be (physical) right (i.e. firm); but used only as denominative from <H3225> (yamiyn) and transitive, to be right-handed or take the right-hand side :- go (turn) to (on, use) the right hand.

Nigh - a primitive root; **to be or come** (causative bring) **near** (for any purpose); euphemism to lie with a woman; as an enemy, **to attack**; religious to worship; causative **to present**; figurative **to adduce [give evidence for] an argument**; by reversal, to stand back :- (make to) **approach** (nigh), bring (forth, hither, near), (cause to) come (hither, near, nigh), give place, go hard (up), (be, draw, go) near (nigh), offer, **overtake**, present, put, stand.

CHAPTER 8

Drama Free Living

Psalm 91:8 (KJV)

8 Only (<u>merely, nothing but</u>) with thine eyes (<u>sight, think</u>) shalt thou behold (<u>look intently; regard with pleasure, favor or care; consider; regard; have respect</u>) and see (<u>consider, discern</u>) the reward (<u>retribution, requital, reciprocation, recompense</u>) of the wicked (<u>guilty, ungodly, to disturb, violate, condemn, vex, wicked</u>).

In yesterday's study, we had a picture painted for us of being one of the 800 survivors in New York City after a calamity destroyed the other 7,999,200 inhabitants. People to the right and left of us fallen dead. In the earlier verses, we learned that this level of protection is due to God's cover over us.

This is a place of protection God has us for us; we are hidden in plain view. A contradiction for sure, but with God as our protection, we begin to see all sorts of miraculous happenings when we find ourselves in a hard place.

We see that even those who consistently get their flu shots are off work for a couple of weeks every year. Contrast that with our life; we depend on the power of God and the anointing he has given us, to act as an invisible covering that allows us to walk free from sickness year after year.

We see that when people come out against us with harmful words they are proven wrong, sometimes within the moment they open their mouths and sometimes after a time of proving. We see that those who come to us with deceptions meant to swindle us and part us from our money are proven to be untrustworthy as we consult and wait on an answer from Him.

We see folks out there who live in so much drama. If it is not one bad thing it is another, fleeting relationships always gone awry, never enough money, arguing and sputtering in the family, and continual complaining about work. There was a long period in my life that looked like that. But when I began to understand the things I am showing here, my life became drama free over time because of this covering.

It is not to say drama doesn't ever attempt to visit. Instead, the truth of the matter is we always have a choice. The longer I am a part of this, the more I understand that we have much more choice in even the circumstances that come into our lives. However, we do not always control circumstance and what it brings to us, and in that case our choice is how we deal with it. We can choose whether to allow it to become a drama or not.

In this verse, we are told that only narrowly will we be affected by the destruction of the forces that come against us. The word translated "only with" means something very narrow, merely, nothing but. The word translated eyes mean just that; eyes, sight or thought. He uses three words in a row that speak of sight. These words speak of both physical and mental sight.

The definitions reveal meanings like consider, regard with pleasure, discern and visions. Visions are mind/sight experiences. We know enough about God by now that if he meant that we would experience the backlash of this devastation in any other way, he would mention it here. But, no, instead it appears that we are being told that ONLY with our eyes will we see the penalty of the forces that come against us.

If he meant that we would get messy in the process, He would say it here. If we felt physical or emotional pain in this, He would have said it. If there would be harm to us in any aspect of our being, or even the things that pertain to us; He would have said it.

And so what will we see? Well, it says that we will regard with pleasure, we will consider, we see the reward coming back to the wicked that they were attempting to do to us. The wicked means the morally wrong, those intending to harm us, those who disturb our peace of mind and those who continually throw roadblocks up to our projects and progress.

This doesn't mean that every person who comes against us will fall to the ground dead. But it does mean that when people sow negative things in our direction, they will receive back a crop or harvest in that which they attempted to clutter our life. If a person (and we remember that they are not our true enemy, but there are spiritual forces using them to work against us) is vexing us, creating some disturbance that they are trying to draw us into; their retribution or payback would be a disturbance of like kind in their life.

This aligns with a seed time/harvest time. The idea of "you reap what you sow." Other people out there call this Karma. I call it protection from God.

Good morning, Father. Thank you for relieving us of the pressure of worry. When we realize that our life is protected in this manner the burden that comes with worry dissipates, vanishing into thin air. We thank you for the all-encompassing coverage that your protection gives. There is not one area of our life that this does not entail. We ask that this understanding is expanded for us and that we lean on you for protection in all aspects of our lives. We receive this favor with joy and gladness, so much so that others may look in wonder at our calm in the face of the turmoil brewing in the world today and wonder how, wonder why. We ask that when they see us operating in peace that they come to us and that we can direct them to you. We pray for not only the small day to day elements of our personal lives but; ask for peace in Israel, in Jerusalem. In Jesus' name, we praise and thank you....Amen!

Definitions used for today's study:
Only with – the same as <H7534> (raq) as a noun; properly leanness, i.e. (figurative) limitation; **only** adverbial **merely**, or conjunctive although :- but, even, except, howbeit, howsoever, at the least, nevertheless, nothing but, notwithstanding, only, save, so [that], surely, yet (so), in any wise; from <H7556> (raqaq) in its orig. **sense**; emaciated (as if flattened out) :- lean ([-fleshed]), thin. a primitive root; **to spit** :- spit.

Eyes - probably a primitive word; **an eye** (literal or figurative); by analogy a fountain (as the eye of the landscape) :- affliction, outward appearance, + before, + think best, colour, conceit, + be content, countenance, + displease, eye ([brow], [-d], -sight), face, + favour, fountain, furrow [from the margin], × him, + humble, knowledge, look, (+ well), × me, open (-ly), + (not) please, presence, + regard, resemblance, **sight**, × thee, × them, + **think**, × us, well, × you (-rselves).

Behold - a primitive root; **to scan**, i.e. **look intently** at; by implication to **regard with pleasure, favor or care** :- (cause to) behold, **consider**, look (down), regard, have respect, see.

See - a primitive root; **to see**, literal or figurative (in numerous applications, direct and implied, transitive, intransitive and causative) :- advise self, appear, approve, behold, × certainly, consider, discern, (make to) enjoy, have experience, gaze, take heed, × indeed, × joyfully, lo, look (on, one another, one on another, one upon another, out, up, upon), mark, meet, × be near, perceive, present, provide, regard, (have) respect, (fore-, cause to, let) see (-r, -m, one another), shew (self), × sight of others, (e-) spy, stare, × surely, × think, view, visions.

Reward - feminine of <H7966> (shilluwm); **retribution-punishment that someone deserves, a justly deserved penalty, the act of taking revenge [harming someone in retaliation for something harmful that they have done]**:- recompense; or shillum, shil-loom'; from <H7999> (shalam); **a requital-returning in kind**, i.e. (secure) retribution, (venal) a fee :- recompense, reward; a primitive root; to be safe (in mind, body or estate); figurative to be (causative make) completed; by implication to be friendly; by extension to reciprocate (in various applications) :- make amends, (make an) end, finish, full, give again, make good, (re-) pay (again), (make) (to) (be at) peace (-able), that is perfect, perform, (make) prosper (-ous), recompense, render, requite, make restitution, restore, reward, × surely.

Wicked - from <H7561> (rasha`); **moral wrong**; concrete an (actively) bad person :- + condemned, **guilty**, **ungodly**, wicked (man), that did wrong; a primitive root; to be (causative do or declare) wrong; by implication **to disturb- to interrupt someone and stop them from continuing what they were doing, destroy the peace or tranquility of, change the arrangement or position of**, violate- act in disregard of laws and rules :- **condemn- pronounced or proved guilty**, make trouble, **vex- to make someone annoyed, confused, or worried, disturb the peace of mind of; afflict with mental agitation or distress**, be (commit, deal, depart, do) **wicked- morally wrong and deliberately intending to hurt people, having committed unrighteous acts** (-ly, -ness).

CHAPTER 9

Confident Words Spoken, Head of the Class

Psalm 91:9 (KJV)

9 Because thou hast made (<u>appoint, put, consider, regard</u>) the LORD, which is my refuge (<u>a shelter, trust, flee for protection, to confide in, have hope</u>), even the most High, thy habitation (<u>and abode, home, retreat/asylum, dwell together, a marriage</u>);

In the Interlinear Bible, a couple of Hebrew words are shown at the beginning of this sentence. Those two words are "For you." And so, the Scripture with these two Hebrew words added looks like this "For you, the Lord are my refuge; the Most High made thy habitation." The first translation makes it look like we have chosen God the Highest God a place we run to for protection and our home; a place of relationship from a third person perspective.

In the second translation, it is shown as a statement of confidence. This statement declares God as trustworthy, a place of refuge and the protective benefits in this relationship from the first person status. For you are my refuge and home. For you are my place of trust and hope where we dwell together. For you are my protection, my retreat and asylum from trouble.

It is amazing how wonderful it feels and how freeing it becomes when something bad has begun to threaten our lives, and we speak these words into the face of the adversity. Words have such power and we see evidence of this when we speak these words. These words make you feel fearless, and within that confidence you become fearless.

At the beginning of my walk with God, I wasn't working a full-time job. I had ample time on my hands from May to early August and then got a temp position. I have told you the whole story before and won't go into it now. But I will refresh your memory.

I started a temp position, and my supervisors allowed me to study the Bible five or more hours a day every day. This continued every month I was there. This was truly a gift from God. In that time, I searched for the promises I had heard my early teachers teach. I then compiled them into what I lovingly called my "Satan Buster." It is a collection of scriptures that cover protection, healing, grace, favor, prosperity and peace. I still have it sitting on my side table and reference it often.

I heard from my teachers the power of me speaking these life giving, protection bearing, seed sowing words over my life daily. And I did it. I ran through the whole "Satan Buster" first thing in the morning while getting ready for work. I took it with me and had it on my desk; flipping through the pages between tasks. Of course, I wasn't able to speak it out loud, but would whisper it or with focus read the words of one verse at a time.

Each scripture was followed by "this is the word of God, I believe it and I receive it." In the evening, while watching television, I would hit the mute button during every advertisement and say aloud one or two scriptures. By the end of the day I had run through the "Buster"' three or four times. I had years of wrong thinking and bad living to turn around. If I had not been focused in my pursuit, I would have fallen away.

In our finalized confession based on the protection offered in this Psalm, this verse will show up as a powerful statement of owning refuge or protection from anything negative that attempts to sidetrack our day/our life. The more you say this, the more deeply it will be embedded in your mind and heart and, the more you will see evidence of the protection promised working for you and your family.

Good morning, Father. Thank you for your word and the power that it holds. Thank you for its life giving quality and its ability to change us from the least likely to succeed to head of the class. Thank you for our marriage to you as the word habitation speaks of, how we do become one and operate as an extension of you in the earth. We not only thank you for an escape from all trouble, but ask for an open heart to operate in the highest form possible. We desire to move forward in our understanding of all things 'You' and how our ability to move and influence in our circles is affected by our relationship. We ask that you honor us with opportunities to serve today and thank you for the resources to do so. We look to you for the protection and peace of Jerusalem, that Israel will prevail. In Jesus' name, we praise and thank you….Amen!

Definitions used in today's study:

Made - or siym, seem; a primitive root; to put (used in a great variety of applications, literal, figurative, inference and elliptis) :- × any wise, **appoint**, bring, call [a name], care, cast in, change, charge, commit, **consider**, convey, determine, + disguise, dispose, do, get, give, heap up, hold, impute, lay (down, up), leave, look, make (out), mark, + name, × on, ordain, order, + paint, place, preserve, purpose, put (on), + **regard**, rehearse, reward, (cause to) set (on, up), shew, + stedfastly, take, × tell, + tread down, ([over-]) turn, × wholly, work.

Lord - from <H1961> (hayah); (the) **self-Existent or Eternal**; Jehovah, Jewish national name of God :- **Jehovah**, the Lord. Compare <H3050> (Yahh), <H3069> (Yehovih); a primitive root [compare <H1933> (hava')]; **to exist**, i.e. **be** or become, come to pass (always emphatic, and not a mere copula or auxiliary) :- beacon, × altogether, be (-come, accomplished, committed, like), break, cause, come (to pass), do, faint, fall, + follow, happen, × have, last, pertain, quit (one-) self, require, × use.

Refuge - or machceh, makh-seh'; from <H2620> (chacah); **a shelter [a place where you are protected from harm or abuse, a basic human need]** (literal or figurative) :- hope, (place of) refuge, shelter, **trust [confidence]**; a primitive root; **to flee for protection** [compare <H982> (batach)]; figurative **to confide in** :- **have hope [expect and depend on something happening, grounds to believe your desire will be fulfilled],** make refuge, (put) trust.

Most High - from <H5927> (`alah); **an elevation**, i.e. (adjective) **lofty** (comparative); as title, the Supreme :- (Most, on) high (-er, -est), upper (-most); a primitive root; to ascend, intransitive (be high) or active (mount); used in a great variety of senses, primary and secondary, literal and figurative (as follow) :- arise (up), (cause to) ascend up, at once, break [the day] (up), bring (up), (cause to) burn, carry up, cast up, + shew, climb (up), (cause to, make to) come (up), cut off, dawn, depart, exalt, excel, fall, fetch up, get up, (make to) go (away, up), grow (over), increase, lay, leap, levy, lift (self) up, light, [make] up, ×

mention, mount up, offer, make to pay, + perfect, prefer, put (on), raise, recover, restore, (make to) rise (up), scale, set (up), shoot forth (up), (begin to) spring (up), stir up, take away (up), work.

Habitation - or ma`iyn, maw-een'; (1 Chron. 4:41), from the same as <H5772> (`ownah); **an abode**, of God (the Tabernacle or the Temple), men (**their home**) or animals (their lair); hence **a retreat** (**asylum**) :- den, dwelling ([-] place), habitation; from an unused root apparently meaning **to dwell together**; (sexual) cohabitation :- **duty of marriage**.

CHAPTER 10

Easy Target or Fully Covered?

Psalm 91:10 (KJV)

10 There shall no evil (<u>adversity, affliction, calamity, distress, grief, harm, hurt, mischief, misery, sorrow, trouble, to spoil, breaking to pieces, displease, punish, vex</u>) befall (<u>contraction in anguish, to approach, seek a quarrel</u>) thee, neither shall any plague (<u>a blow, a spot-leperous person, sore, plague, stricken, stroke, wound, to strike, violently, beat, smite</u>) come nigh (<u>to approach, come near, be at hand, offer, present, produce, make ready, stand, take</u>) thy dwelling (<u>a tent, as clearly conspicuous from a distance, home</u>).

Today we need to look hard at these two lists. The two promises in this verse regarding evil and plague; and we are protected from every element of them. When I hear the word evil, I think and see in my mind's eye a sinister person plotting bad things or the wispy traces of a spirit that wreaks havoc.

Although both of those things have a place in this, we can see by the list below that evil is solid, down-to-earth trouble. It is defined by this list of words and the words mean more that we usually take time to think about.

When I considered the word plague, I thought about the rampant sickness brought on by unclean conditions that when it takes hold in a community can wipe out huge numbers of people. And although this is true, again, it is described as much more.

Both of these words cover nearly every aspect of living. Take a close look. Your mind, your heart, your physical body; your work, your success in business, and your finances; your relationships and spiritual matters; every one of these areas of life is covered in the words below.

We are protected because of our relationship with God; this close covenant relationship (similar to marriage), and also protection from angelic forces that will be discussed over the next couple of days.

We first see that **NO** evil will befall, or approach, or seek a quarrel with us. I will first post the words from the Strong's Concordance and then follow them up with dictionary definitions. This will make it clear to us. Here are some of the words used in the definition of evil:

-   Adversity – a difficult period in your life when you have many problems, a calamitous (causing serious damage, or causing a lot of people to suffer, a dire consequence, being in ruin) event, a state of misfortune or affliction

-   Affliction – an illness, a serious problem, cause of great suffering or distress due to ill health

-   Distress – psychological suffering, extreme physical pain, danger or need, unpleasant situation caused by lack of money, food or other basic needs

- Calamity – event that causes serious damage or suffering

- Grief – a strong feeling of sadness usually because of someone's death, great unhappiness, intense sorrow

- Harm – injury, damage or problems, a change for the worse (note: this can be physical or financial or mental or emotional or spiritual)

- Hurt – mental or physical pain or injury, emotional pain, cause problems that impede success, damage or loss, affect negatively

- Mischief – behavior that causes trouble but not serious harm to others, reckless or malicious behavior causing discomfort or annoyance, the quality of being harmful or evil

- Misery – intense unhappiness, state of ill-being due to misfortune

- Sorrow – great sadness associated with bereavement, wrong doing or disappointment

- Trouble – problems, worries, difficulties; additional or special effort that causes you problems or is inconvenient; a situation for which you are likely to be blamed, criticized, or punished; angry disturbance; feeling of strong anxiety

- Spoil - affected in a way that make worse, less attractive, or less enjoyable; decay; valuables taken by violence; destroy and strip of possessions; hinder or prevent efforts, plans and desires

-   Displease – annoyed and dissatisfied

-   Punish – make someone suffer because they have done something against the rules or something they have done;

-   Vex – make annoyed, confused or worried; subject someone to prolonged examination, discussion, or deliberation; disturb with minor irritations, have mysterious or bewildering situations, change arrangements or position; disturb the peace of mind with agitation or distress

And **NO** plague will come near to, approach, present itself at our homes. These are the words used to define plague:

-   Blow – stops working; destroy chance of succeeding; become unable to use or operate; deplete supply; hit hard with fist or weapon; something that causes sadness, disappointment, shock; cause to be revealed and jeopardized (a special agent)

-   Infliction – cause pain or damage, impose tax or embargo, source of unhappiness or trouble

-   Spot – a dirty mark that should not be there, sign of disease, an act that brings discredit to someone, impaired or flawed

-   Leprosy – serious disease that affects the skin, nerves and bones and can cause fingers and toes to fall off

-   Sore – painful and uncomfortable, angry or offended, injured or infected

- Stricken – affected by serious problems like illness or injury; damaged or destroyed by a bomb, or fire or flood; put out of action

- Wound – injury to skin, emotional damage

- Violently – sudden with great energy or force, a violent manner

- Beat – hit violently, defeat in a game, competition or battle

- Plague – any serious disease that spreads quickly to a lot of people and usually ends in death; an uncontrolled and usually harmful increase in the numbers of an animal or insect; to annoy someone all the time by repeatedly doing or asking

I need to repeat myself, look closely at this list and you will see that it covers nearly every adverse occurrence that could possible come to tamper with peace; health, wealth, relationship issues, emotional, spiritual and physical well-being. The promise to us is that these things will not approach us, seek a quarrel with us, or come near to us.

If it is helpful, print these lists out and use them as a guideline to assess the circumstances that appear in your life. Measure those things that come against you. If they fit any one of these categories, speak to that condition and remind it that you are a child of God. Remind yourself and the angelic host that you know freedom in this area is yours.

Remind the forces of evil they have no quarter in your life at all, and at this minute particularly this area of life.

Command it to leave, and believe God will enforce this part of His own law.

We hear stories of men and women of God, who have been in incidents similar to these dangerous elements, we hear the testimonies of God's hand keeping the safe from the danger. If we stop to think of some of our histories, we could identify times when we were saved from some destruction or physical harm or bad circumstance. I am sure we could all come up with several examples.

Just think of how much more aware we will be the next time we have a near miss or close call, if we begin to speak these protective verses over our lives. Once we become aware of the multitude of circumstances covered by these two little words, our level of anxiety or concern over all of the craziness in the world begins to melt away.

Once we begin to speak God's promise over our lives, our confidence rises. And once the enemy sees that he is no longer able to get us to run for the hills, or quiver with fear, he will begin to bother someone less prepared.

I can't leave out this piece. If you look at the first definition of the word translated as dwelling, the definition starts out with the word tent. But the definition of tent is "as clearly conspicuous from a distance" and the root word is "to shine." Is this perhaps, one of those instances when the word translated and the base of the word don't seem to jive?

Something happens in the spirit world when we have received Jesus as our Savior and walk in this Family as a full-fledged member. We begin to shine, and it becomes clear to those who see us. It is also evident to the enemy, and he often chooses to look for that "half in, half out" believer. Their light is not as bright, and our enemy operates best in shades of darkness.

I say when we walk like a full-fledged member because many who come in don't understand their place. When they don't; their life is not as fulfilled in the natural and chinks seem to be visible in their spiritual armor. We speak and act as if one foot is in the Family, and one foot is out. This gives the enemy access he shouldn't have, to bring trouble to us.

However, let's say we do walk as that adopted child with the same rights as the first-born. When we do, we and our house shines and can be conspicuously seen from a distance. When this verse says that evil and plagues will not approach us, seek a quarrel with us, or come near to us, it is because our spiritual mantle is seen from afar. I leave you with a question today. Why would these messengers of the devil mess with you and your life when there are other folks around you that are easy targets?

Good morning, Father. Thank you for your protection not only of our physical person, but our possessions, our success and our mental, emotional and spiritual well-being. You are the cover for us in all situations. You are a warring husband, on the warpath against any threat to the life and livelihood of his bride. You have chosen to respond to threats against us in this manner, and when we are aware and willing to receive the protection you offer, the enemy has no quarter near us or anything that may be remotely connected to us. We are heirs to this wonderful benefit of our salvation and this loving relationship with you. You originally promised this to our Jewish brothers and sisters, and we continue to stand together in prayer for

Jerusalem.   In Jesus' name, we praise and thank you....Amen!

Definitions used in today's study:

Evil - from <H7489> (ra`a`); bad or (as noun) evil (natural or moral) :- **adversity**, **affliction**, bad, **calamity**, + displease (-ure), **distress**, evil ([-favouredness], man, thing), + exceedingly, × great, **grief** (-vous), **harm**, heavy, **hurt** (-ful), ill (favoured), + mark, **mischief** (-vous), **misery**, naught (-ty), noisome, + not please, sad (-ly), sore, **sorrow**, **trouble**, vex, wicked (-ly, -ness, one), worse (-st), wretchedness, wrong. [Incling feminine ra`ah; as adjective or noun.]; a primitive root; properly **to spoil** (literal by **breaking to pieces**); figurative to make (or be) good for nothing, i.e. bad (physically, socially or morally) :- afflict, associate selves [by mistake for <H7462> (ra`ah)], break (down, in pieces), + displease, (be, bring, do) evil (doer, entreat, man), show self friendly [by mistake for <H7462> (ra`ah)], do harm, (do) hurt, (behave self, deal) ill, × indeed, do mischief, **punish**, still, vex, (do) wicked (doer, -ly), be (deal, do) worse.

Befall - a primitive root [perhaps rather identical with <H578> ('anah) through the idea of **contraction in anguish**]; **to approach**; hence to meet in various senses :- befall, deliver, happen, **seek a quarrel**; a primitive root; to groan :- lament, mourn.

Plague - from <H5060> (naga`); **a blow** (figurative infliction); also (by implication) **a spot (concrete a leprous person or dress**) :- plague, **sore**, **stricken**, stripe, **stroke**, **wound**; a primitive root; properly to touch, i.e. lay the hand upon (for any purpose; euphemism, to lie with a woman); by implication to reach (figurative to arrive, acquire); **violently**, to strike (punish, defeat, destroy, etc.) :- beat, (× be able to) bring (down), cast, come (nigh), draw near (nigh), get up, happen, join, near, plague, reach (up), smite, strike, touch.

Nigh - a primitive root; **to approach** (causative bring near) for whatever purpose :- (cause to) approach, (cause to) bring (forth, near), **(cause to) come (near, nigh)**, (cause to) draw near (nigh), go (near), **be at hand**, join, be near, **offer**, **present**, **produce**, **make ready**, **stand**, **take**.

Dwelling - from <H166> ('ahal); **a tent (as clearly conspicuous from a distance)** :- covering, (dwelling) (place), **home**, tabernacle, tent; a primitive root; to be clear :- shine.

CHAPTER 11

Angels vs. Cherubs, Puppies vs. Rottweilers

Psalm 91:11 (KJV)

11 For he shall give his angels (<u>to dispatch a deputy</u>) charge (<u>establish and give authority to operate, messenger</u>) over thee, to keep (<u>guard, protect, attend-to take care of someone in an important position</u>) thee in all thy ways (<u>course of life or mode of action, conversation, custom, to walk</u>).

Yesterday we learned that we have no need to fear evil and plagues, and all of the various definitions that are contained in these two words. The first reason is that we have decided to make the Lord our refuge (place of protection) and habitation (dwelling or home). The second is that God has assigned angels to protect and minister to us.

Angelic protection is a subject that many people, whether they subscribe to Christian beliefs or not, believe. There are statues and pieces of jewelry, comedic scenes with an angel on one shoulder and a devil on the other, but all of these show angels as small cherub. Cherubs are listed as small, child-like angels with wings, and in Strong's Concordance it calls them imaginary beings.

These cute little angels with a quiver of arrows dipped in a love potion are quite different from the angels of God. As warm and fuzzy as these little round faces may make you feel initially; I liken the difference between the idea of angels versus the reality of them, to the difference between a newborn puppy and a full grown, on-guard Rottweiler or Doberman pinscher.

I don't know about the struggles you have had, but I have had plenty when there would have been no comfort thinking I had the protection of one of these soft cuddly puppies.

I want a protector that knows how to take orders and fulfill them. I want a protector who can think on their feet and be prepared to switch directions at a moment's notice. I want a strong, agile protector with the ability to give me comfort and show me love (in this case the love of God). And yet, when facing an enemy of mine will stand between me and the trouble; muscles rippling beneath the surface, teeth bared (swords drawn), growling (speaking in a thunderous angelic language) to warn off the perpetrators.

I want a protector who is ready to engage with a moment's notice. Angels are those ambassadors. They represent Him in a protective role for our lives. They are efficient and prompt deputies sent to act with the power of God. They hedge us about to keep us in safety, they have been established to function as messengers from God to us.

They are a combination of gentleman's gentleman and a body guard, delivering messages and necessities from our

Father and carrying out orders of protection. What an awesome combination and wonderful comfort.

Good morning, Father. Thank you for angels that are realer than the chair I am sitting in. Thank you for knowing there is not a breath we take when our body guards are not present. Thank you that we understand that they are not only protective spirits, but are ministering spirits as well, we understand that they hearken not only to God's direction but the words of our voice. Activation comes when we speak. Unfortunately, many of us do not give them anything to do, as our minds and hearts are often consumed with negative thought and our mouths speaks out things that do not align with God's word. But as of today, we chose to be active participants in our precept driven lives. We chose to guage every thought and word, speaking only those things that align with the promises of God. In doing so, we activate the angelic host around us with our words, which will protect us in our walk and will deliver to us whatever message or material stuff we need to fulfill the tasks of today. We ask for open eyes to see the need of others around us, and the heart to help. We pray for the peace of Jerusalem, the protection of Israel. In Jesus' name, we praise and thank you....Amen!

Definitions used for today's study:
Angels - from an unused root meaning **to despatch [the act of sending off, the property as of efficient and prompt] as a deputy [someone whose job is the second most important in a department or organization, an assistant with power to act when his superior is absent]**; a messenger; specifically of God, i.e. **an angel (also a prophet, priest or teacher)** :- **ambassador**

[a senior official who lives in a foreign country and represents his or her own country there], angel, king, messenger.

Charge - a primitive root; (intensive) **to constitute [establish and give authority to operate, charge with a task or function]**, enjoin :- appoint, (for-) bid, (give a) charge, (give a, give in, send with) command (-er, -ment), send a messenger, put, (set) in order.

Keep - a primitive root; properly **to hedge about (as with thorns)**, i.e. **guard**; generally **to protect**, **attend to**, etc. :- beware, be circumspect, take heed (to self), keep (-er, self), mark, look narrowly, **observe [watch attentively]**, **preserve [keep in safety and protect from harm, decay, loss, or destruction]**, regard, reserve, save (self), sure, (that lay) wait (for), watch (-man).

Ways - from <H1869> (darak); **a road** (as trodden); figurative a **course of life or mode of action**, often adverb :- along, away, because of, + by, conversation, custom, [east-] ward, journey, manner, passenger, through, toward, [high-] [path-] way [-side], whither [-soever]; a primitive root; to tread; by implication **to walk**; also to string a bow (by treading on it in bending) :- archer, bend, come, draw, go (over), guide, lead (forth), thresh, tread (down), walk.

CHAPTER 12

You're In Good Hands

Psalm 91:12 (KJV)

12 They shall bear (lift up, bring forth, carry away, fetch, take away) thee up in their hands (the hollow hand or palm, figuratively power, to bow down), lest thou dash (to push, gore, defeat, hurt, stub the toe, stumble, put to the worse) thy foot against a stone.

Have you ever been walking along minding your own business and all of a sudden you are down on the ground? It has happened to me a couple of times in my life. The first time I was busy walking forward, with my head turned around and talking to some of my classmates when a concrete step got in my way. Smash! My chin hit the top of three steps; I brushed myself off and acted like nothing had happened.

Well, I acted like I was all right until several people, through looks of horror and concern came up asking if I was okay. I realized that I was bleeding profusely from a gaping wound in my chin. What a mess it was. Several stitches later, pounding headache, a bruised mouth, and ego; and I was back on my way. But, it took several weeks to heal completely from the incident.

The second time happened forty years later. I had just moved into a new apartment with an attached garage. The garage was a pretty tight fit, so that when I pulled in face first getting around the front was a bit of a squeeze. I had dropped by the store and picked up some groceries. In front of the door, there is a piece of carpeting as a mat to wipe your feet on before entering.

Purse in hand and no fewer than three bags of groceries hanging off my arms and in hands to eliminate more trips out to the car; I sidled through the space between the car and some storage bins. My vision was severely limited with so much in my hands and then, my toe caught the edge of that carpet. Next thing I knew I was on top of several empty boxes from the move with groceries all over the garage floor.

Fortunately this time I had only a couple bruises on my legs and a very badly bruised forearm. Although I was by myself, and no one could see which saved my pride, the bruises were deep and took several weeks before the bruised forearm wasn't hollering at me every time I typed at work. These are both scenarios in which having an angelic hand come in and scoop me up would have been great; looking back, both incidences could have ended much worse.

I think you can see by these two examples that I was the real source of the problem. Now I am not saying that there weren't obstacles there, but was it the obstacle or the lack of focus that tripped me up? I could try to blame that step or piece of carpet. However, in one situation it was my lack of paying attention to where I was going and in the other, a lack of focus along with trying to do too much at one time that created the real problem.

There are many published miraculous accounts of angelic intervention when a person has escaped physical injury that seemed imminent, and I would never discount the possibility of that happening. This verse it is not clear whether we are speaking in physical or figurative terms, so let's assume the widest available coverage available to us.

This verse is saying that the angels assigned to us will lift us up and carry us away from the obstacles we face in life. The stone seems to be an all-inclusive term for an obstacle or problem. Fill in the blank with an issue that you are facing. Sometimes we are aware of the challenges that face us, and sometimes the root of the problem goes unseen.

This protection covers those thing seen and unseen by us. This protection covers anything that could "dash" us; being pushed, gored, defeated (temporarily), inflicted with disease, or anything that would put us to the worse.

Good morning, Father. Thank you for giving us these angelic hands that lift us out and away from trouble. These protectors have kept us from all manner of physical trouble. We can't possibly see all that is coming against us in our day to day activities. We choose to believe that their protection extends to whatever need, whatever obstacle we face. As this works for us, we believe it does for all of your people. We continue our prayer cover for Jerusalem, and the Hebrew people. Besides these, please give us eyes to see and a heart to act for those you place in our path today. In Jesus' name, we pray....Amen!

Definitions used on today's study:

Bear thee up - or nacah, naw-saw'; (Psa. 4:6 [7]), a primitive root; **to lift**, in a great variety of applications, literal and figurative, absolutely and relatively (as follows) :- accept, advance, arise, (able to, [armour], suffer to) bear (-er, up), bring (forth), burn, **carry (away)**, cast, contain, desire, ease, exact, exalt (self), extol, fetch, forgive, furnish, further, give, go on, help, high, hold up, honourable (+ man), lade, lay, **lift (self) up**, lofty, marry, magnify, × needs, obtain, pardon, raise (up), receive, regard, respect, set (up), spare, stir up, + swear, take (away, up), × utterly, wear, yield.

Hands - from <H3721> (kaphaph); **the hollow hand or palm** (so of the paw of an animal, of the sole, and even of the bowl of a dish or sling, the handle of a bolt, the leaves of a palm-tree); **figurative power** :- branch, + foot, hand ([-ful], -dle, [-led]), hollow, middle, palm, paw, power, sole, spoon; a primitive root; to curve :- bow down (self).

Dash - a primitive root; **to push**, **gore**, **defeat**, stub (the toe), inflict (a disease) :- beat, dash, hurt, plague, slay, smite (down), strike, stumble, × surely, put to the worse.

Foot - from <H7270> (ragal); **a foot** (as used in walking); by implication a step; by euphemism the pudenda :- × be able to endure, × according as, × after, × coming, × follow, ([broken-]) foot ([-ed, -stool]), × great toe, × haunt, × journey, leg, + piss, + possession, time; a primitive root; to walk along; but only in specifically applications, to reconnoitre, to be a tale-bearer (i.e. slander); also (as denominative from <H7272> (regel)) to lead about :- backbite, search, slander, (e-) spy (out), teach to go, view.

Stone - from the root of <H1129> (banah) through the meaning **to build**; **a stone** :- + carbuncle, + mason, + plummet, [chalk-, hail-, head-, sling-] stone (-ny), (divers) weight (-s); a primitive root; to build (literal and figurative) :- (begin to) build (-er), obtain children, make, repair, set (up), × surely.

CHAPTER 13

The Oppressor or The Oppressed?

Psalm 91:13 (KJV)

[13] Thou shalt tread (to walk, to string a bow by treading on it in bending) upon the lion (to roar) and adder (to twist, any clever, deceptive maneuver, unforeseen development): the young lion (a village as covered in walls, a young lion covered in a mane) and the dragon (a marine or land monster, abnormally large and powerful) shalt thou trample (to tread upon, an oppressor, someone who subjects others to undue pressure) under feet.

This protection chapter not only discusses the role of God's protection, the protection of our angelic forces but also our role in safety. If you pay attention, this verse is stating that we have power, too.

Throughout the Old Testament, people who walked in faith operated in a confidence that God backed their decisions and movements. In New Testament times, we have a power that is called the anointing. Therefore, we don't typically walk in that power to its full capacity. It is not entirely understood, but we study in order to understand.

This verse tells us that we will tread on, bend to our need, guide, lead forth the enemies of our life. It was written when there was only the promise of the Messiah. This was many years before Jesus was seen by the people, years before his power was transferred to believers (by being engrafted into the family).

The enemies spoken about, bring to mind many aspects of human behavior. The lion is the animal that we have come to know as the king of the jungle. They roar and they are fierce among other things. As these two words are used in the definition, we will look at these. Roaring is to say something in a loud, deep, angry voice. Anger is often an enemy we have to face, and it is one that many become intimidated by it.

Fierce has many of the same aspects; violently agitated and turbulent, involving very strong feelings such as determination, anger, or hate, ready to attack. It is one of those forces that come against us in every circle, and if we lack confidence, we cower rather than standing strong. The adder is from a root word meaning to twist and contort.

Further description of these words means a jerky pulling movement, clever or deceptive maneuvers, and unseen developments. The word for a young lion speaks of covering; like a mane on the head and neck of a lion, or the walls of a village. A dragon is described as someone or something that is abnormally large and powerful, a jackal a wild, vicious dog.

Any one of these things could be looked at as if it were one of the many attacks of the enemy. We have people, and situations that are fierce and angry. Some people twist and contort the truth until it looks different than originally intended. There are unforeseen developments popping up daily.

Politically correct oppression can be seen by overlooking or approving behavior that most folks, and the Word of God, believes is wrong. If you don't succumb to popular social thought you are wrongly marked as being bigoted and hard hearted, which is another form of intimidation.

There are things that happen in our lives that feel like they will tear us apart as a wild jackal; or are so abnormally big that we feel like we will be swallowed up and never seen again.

Yet, this verse tells us we can step on them and bend them just like we do when stringing a bow. It says that we can walk on top of and not under the influence of them. We will tread or press or crush under our feet these threats to our peace.

It says that we will thresh, or give a thrashing to; beat hard those things that come against us. And it says that we will do so with our feet. We are the ones with authority to oppress the opposition. It is our place to place undue pressure on them, not the other way around.

As this was written many years before Jesus came on the scene and people who were in league with God had this power then, how much more does this pertain to us today? Isn't it time for us to quit living in fear?

Good morning, Father. Thank you for helping us to understand that we are co-workers in our own protection. As is stated in so many other areas of the Bible, we have authority in this world. This authority is reinforced with our voice. When we speak these God-given words over our lives it acts as a reminder in the spiritual world, and it builds confidence in our mind and heart. We speak protection over ourselves, family, friends and associates. And Lord, we pray for the peace of Jerusalem. In Jesus' name, we praise and thank you....Amen!

Definitions used in today's study:

Tread - a primitive root; **to tread**; by implication **to walk**; also **to string a bow (by treading on it in bending)**:- archer, bend, come, draw, go (over), guide, lead (forth), thresh, tread (down), walk.

Lion - from an unused root probably meaning **to roar**; a lion (from his characteristic *roar*) :- (fierce) lion.

Adder - from an unused root meaning **to twist [a jerky pulling movement; any clever (deceptive) maneuver; an unforeseen development]** ; **an asp (from its contortions)** :- adder.

Young lion - from <H3722> (kaphar); **a *village* (as *covered* in by walls)**; also **a young lion (perhaps as covered with a mane)** :- (young) lion, village. Compare <H3723> (kaphar); a primitive root; **to *cover*** (specifically with bitumen); figurative to **expiate [to show that you are sorry for something bad you have done by doing something good]** or **condone [to approve of behavior that most people think is wrong; excuse, overlook, or make allowances for; be lenient with]** , to *placate* or *cancel* :- appease, make (an) atonement, cleanse, disannul, forgive, be merciful, pacify, pardon, purge (away), put off, (make) reconcile (-liation)

Dragon - or tanniym, tan-neem'; (Ezek. 29:3), intensive from the same as <H8565> (tan); **a marine or land monster [someone or something that is abnormally large and powerful]**, i.e. sea-serpent or jackal :- dragon, sea-monster, serpent, whale; from an unused root probably meaning to elongate; a monster (as preternaturally formed), i.e. a sea-serpent (or other huge marine animal); also a jackal (or other hideous land animal) :- dragon, whale. Compare <u><H8577></u> (tanniyn).

Feet - a primitive root; **to *tread* upon** (as a potter, in walking or abusively) :- **oppressor [a person of authority who subjects others to undue pressures]**, **stamp upon**, **trample (under feet)**, **tread (down, upon)**.

CHAPTER 14

Our Love is Discovered by Seeing

Psalm 91:14 (KJV)

[14] Because he hath set his love (cling, join, delight in) upon me, therefore will I deliver (escape, deliver, carry away safe) him: I will set him on high (lofty, especially inaccessible, safe, strong), because he hath known (observation, care, recognition, ascertain by seeing) my name (through the idea of definite and conspicuous position, a mark or memorial of individuality, honor, authority, character, renown) .

The power and authority we spoke about yesterday is a benefit of the love relationship we have with God. "Because he has set his love upon me...." He carries us to safety from any and all problems. He set us on high according to these definitions in a place that is strong, safe, and especially inaccessible.

Our love relationship starts with His unfailing love. 1 John 4:19 (KJV) says it this way, "We love him, because he first loved us." It is a love that we can't fully understand, try as we might. But little by little, especially as we see evidence of this love played out in our lives, we begin to trust.

In that trusting, warm affection grows. Then, the more we allow ourselves to rely on Him in even the harshest situations, the greater and greater levels of grace we see played out. He piles on, heaps on us, an overabundance of supply in whatever area our need is. The more we see this played out in our behalf, the more our warm affection grows into a full-blown love. Here it is spoken of as known, or observed, or ascertained by seeing.

This is a love we would fight for. We stand up for our husband or wife when someone slanders them. In the same way does this feeling begin to grow for Him. You might fight with your sister or brother, but let someone outside the family come against them, and you are ready to defend to the end. You would give your life to save theirs.

But even these earthly loves are flawed and with flawed people come flawed relationships. God's love for us is not flawed, and perfect in every sense.

This love is already available on the other side of this relationship before we enter into it. The thing we don't really know is how to deal with such love. We often don't trust it because of the hurts we accumulate over the years. The hurts coming from outside of our families make more sense, but many start at home. Many of us come from a one-parent home or a blended family. In these cases, there often was not a full-time father or mother; this can generate feelings of abandonment and betrayal.

I just had a conversation with a new friend about how we can trust God, when so many of us weren't in a position to trust an earthly father, or mother, or loving authority figure. But, God is patient. He understands the harm we've experienced in relationships, in the past. He is willing to work from a place of distrust to trust; from a place of running from Him to running to Him for cover; from a shaky to a solid friendship; and from a place of warm affection to fierce loyalty and love.

As we flow from one level of this relationship to the next, understanding the Name of the Lord in all its aspects becomes clearer. With each revelation of His Name and the blessing that comes with it, the more solid our confidence is in this elevated position He gives us. But does this mean that this elevated place of safety, this especially inaccessible spot of protection is withheld until we fully love Him? No! Our place is secure with the acceptance of Jesus as our Savior.

Good morning, Father. Thank you for the love you first gave us. Thank you for showing us this love in the fact that Jesus gave his life for ours. Thank you for the blanket of not just fatherly love, but warm affection you have for us. As is with our earthly relationships, we grow into love with you. Gratefully you don't withhold our benefit as your child while you are waiting for us to fall fully in love with you. No! This was written and promised to those who didn't yet know Jesus. With his work we can consider that it is indeed finished, we are covered. Father, we stand with our brothers and sisters over the world in praying for the peace of Jerusalem. Protect and prosper them. In Jesus' name, we praise and thank you….Amen!

Definitions used in today's study:
Love - a primitive root; to **cling**, i.e. **join**, (figurative) **to love, delight in**; elliptical (or by interchanging for <H2820> (chasak))

to deliver :- have a delight, (have a) desire, fillet, long, set (in) love.

Deliver - a primitive root; to slip out, i.e. **escape**; causative to **deliver** :- calve, **carry away safe**, deliver, (cause to) escape.

High - a primitive root; **to be** (causative *make*) **lofty, especially inaccessible**; by implication **safe, strong**; used literal and figurative :- **defend**, exalt, be excellent, (be, set on) high, lofty, be safe, set up (on high), be too strong.

Known - a primitive root; **to know (properly to ascertain by seeing)**; used in a great variety of senses, figurative, literal, euphemism and inference (including **observation, care, recognition**; and causative instruction, designation, punishment, etc.) [as follow] :- acknowledge, acquaintance (-ted with), advise, answer, appoint, assuredly, be aware, [un-] awares, can [-not], certainly, for a certainty, comprehend, consider, × could they, cunning, declare, be diligent, (can, cause to) discern, discover, endued with, familiar friend, famous, feel, can have, be [ig-] norant, instruct, kinsfolk, kinsman, (cause to, let, make) know, (come to give, have, take) knowledge, have [knowledge], (be, make, make to be, make self) known, + be learned, + lie by man, mark, perceive, privy to, × prognosticator, regard, have respect, skilful, shew, can (man of) skill, be sure, of a surety, teach, (can) tell, understand, have [understanding], × will be, wist, wit, wot.

Name - a primitive word [perhaps rather from <H7760> (suwm) **through the idea of definite and conspicuous position**; compare <H8064> (shamayim)]; **an appellation, as a mark or memorial of individuality**; by implication **honor, authority, character** :- + base, [in-] fame [-ous], name (-d), **renown**, report.

CHAPTER 15

Expectant Urgency vs. Frantic Pleading

Psalm 91:15 (KJV)

15 He shall call (to accost, stop someone and speak to them especially in a way that is annoying or embarrassing) upon me, and I will answer (see and heed or pay close attention to, respond to) him: I will be with him in trouble(scarcity of money, shortage of credit, only just enough, so little time it is difficult to do what needs to be done, firmly in a particular position, being squeezed, nervous or annoyed, rigid, invulnerable to penetration, difficult to handle or beat through cleverness and with, demands of strict rules/procedures); I will deliver (to pull off, to depart, to equip for fight, strengthen, arm man/soldier), him, and honor (to be heavy in in a good sense, numerous, rich, honorable, abounding with, glorious [bringing great happiness and thankfulness], promote, to honor [a tangible symbol signifying approval or distinction, bestow rewards upon, show respect]) him.

I couldn't help but giggle at the first definition of the word translated as the word call. Although there are other less forceful definitions as properly address by name, bidden, cry unto, preach, proclaim, pronounce, and publish; the first definition is "through the idea of accosting." Accosting means to stop someone and speak to them especially in a way that is annoying or embarrassing.

Why would a person approach and talk to someone this way? More importantly why would a person approach and talk to God this way? I guess we could look at other questions that might help us get to the answer. When was the last time that you were in some deep trouble? How did you feel? Some insight is found in the definitions for trouble that could help us.

Trouble is defined with words like scarcity, squeezed, rigidity, nervous, annoyed, fastened in position, situations that are difficult to handle or beat through cleverness, and the demands of strict rules/procedures (laws); adversity, affliction, anguish, distress, and tribulation.

Unless you have gone through a few of the "fire drills" of life and have seen God's hand at work to remove the threat of these situations, your lack of experience can heighten the fear brought about by trouble. The pressure felt when going through any one of the physical, emotional or circumstantial conditions that "trouble" indicates, will usually bring discomfort.

Pressure or stress usually sets a person's emotions on edge. The less sure you are of God's intent to be your protective cover, the more panicked your conversation with Him may be. Your request for assistance might be frantic and pleading.

But what if we look at this with a different light? What if we say this person is fully aware of God's promise and desire to protect? The difference in the approach taken with the request is not in the force of the delivery (the call);

instead, the difference is in the expectancy that this is the one person that can be counted on and will respond with whatever is needed to resolve the issue. The urgency is there; the panic is not. The expectancy is evident; frantic pleading is a thing of the past.

Once the "call" is made to God, his promise is to deliver and honor us. The word translated as deliver in this verse is different from the one used in verse :14. That definition was "to slip out, escape, carry away safe." The definition for the word used today is to pull off (be successful or achieve a goal, remove by pulling), to equip for a fight, strengthen, arm self, armed man/soldier, make fat, ready or prepare.

The definition used yesterday is clearly providing a means of escape and carrying away to safety. But the definition in this verse speaks far more about us being equipped for a fight, preparation for readiness, strengthened and ultimately succeeding or achieving a goal that the trouble was attempting to thwart. Once again, we have been assigned as a co-worker with God in our protection.

This successful mission or the achieved goal is the honor provided to us by our God. Honor speaks of heaviness in a good way. It is something that can be seen by others. It is rich and abundant. It is glorious in that it brings great happiness and thankfulness. It is a God promotion with tangible symbols signifying approval and distinction for us, with the added bonus of rewards and respect.

Good morning, Father. Thank you for understanding that coming to you and making requests can take many forms. In the beginning, we may have a sense of panic when faced by trouble, and as we grow in our relationship with you that panic is replaced by a fervent expectancy. We may not know the answer, but know you have one. And as proven out by these two verses, deliverance can come in the form of you snatching us away from trouble or equipping us with the tools and plan to navigate the problem and triumph. We are exceedingly grateful for the honor provided by You, knowing that when we are distinguished it is a reflection of you for others to see. With all these gifts, we ask that you show us who we can be of service to today. In Jesus' name, we praise and thank you....Amen!

Definitions used for today's study:
Call - a primitive root [rather identical with <H7122> (qara') **through the idea of accosting [to stop someone and speak to them, especially in a way that could annoy them or make them feel embarrassed] a person met**]; to call out to (i.e. properly address by name, but used in a wide variety of applications) :- bewray [self], that are bidden, call (for, forth, self, upon), cry (unto), (be) famous, guest, invite, mention, (give) name, preach, (make) proclaim (-ation), pronounce, publish, read, renowned, say; a primitive root; to encounter, whether accidentally or in a hostile manner :- befall, (by) chance, (cause to) come (upon), fall out, happen, meet.

Answer - a primitive root; properly **to eye or (general) to heed**, i.e. **pay attention**; by implication **to respond**; by extension to begin to speak; specifically to sing, shout, testify, announce :- give account, afflict [by mistake for <H6031> (`anah)], (cause to, give) answer, bring low [by mistake for <H6031> (`anah)], cry, hear, Leannoth, lift up, say, × scholar, (give a) shout, sing (together by course), speak, testify, utter, (bear) witness. See also <H1042> (Beyth `Anowth), <H1043> (Beyth `Anath).

Trouble - feminine of <H6862> (tsar); **tightness [lack of movement or room for movement, a state occasioned by scarcity of money and a shortage of credit, you have only just**

enough, you have so little time that it is difficult for you to do what you need to, firmly fastened in a particular position, being squeezed, nervous or annoyed, rigid, invulnerable to penetration, affected by scarcity and expensive to borrow, exasperatingly difficult to handle or circumvent, demanding strict attention to rules and procedures] (i.e. figurative trouble); transitive a female rival :- **adversary**, **adversity**, **affliction**, **anguish**, **distress**, **tribulation**, trouble; or tsar, tsawr; from <H6887> (tsarar); narrow; (as a noun) a tight place (usually figurative, i.e. trouble); also a pebble (as in <H6864> (tsor)); (transitive) an opponent (as crowding) :- adversary, afflicted (-tion), anguish, close, distress, enemy, flint, foe, narrow, small, sorrow, strait, tribulation, trouble; a primitive root; to cramp, literal or figurative, transitive or intransitive (as follows) :- adversary, (be in) afflict (-ion), besiege, bind (up), (be in, bring) distress, enemy, narrower, oppress, pangs, shut up, be in a strait (trouble), vex.

Deliver - a primitive root; **to pull off**; hence (intensive) to strip, (reflexive) to depart; by implication to deliver, **equip (for fight)**; present, **strengthen** :- **arm (self)**, (go, ready) armed (× man, soldier), deliver, draw out, **make fat**, loose, (ready) prepared, put off, take away, withdraw self.

Honour - or kabed, kaw-bade'; a primitive root; **to be heavy**, i.e. in a bad sense (burdensome, severe, dull) or **in a good sense (numerous, rich, honorable)**; causative to make weighty (in the same two senses) :- **abounding with**, more grievously afflict, boast, be chargeable, × be dim, glorify, be (make) **glorious [bringing great happiness and thankfulness]** (things), glory, (very) great, be grievous, harden, be (make) heavy, be heavier, lay heavily, (bring to, come to, do, get, be had in) honour (self), (be) honourable (man), lade, × more be laid, make self many, nobles, prevail, **promote (to honour{a tangible symbol signifying approval or distinction, bestow rewards upon, show respect]),** be rich, be (go) sore, stop.

CHAPTER 16

Making a Pig of Yourself

Psalm 91:16 (KJV)

16 With long (<u>forever, draw out, lengthen</u>) life (<u>days, full, life, process of time</u>) will I satisfy (<u>sate – fill to satisfaction, have plenty, be satiate – overeat or eat immodestly or make a pig of oneself, be sufficient or adequate in quality or quantity</u>) him, and show (<u>to see, view, present, prove</u>) him my salvation (<u>something saved, deliverance, victory, prosperity, health, help, welfare, to free, succor-assist in time of difficulty or serious need, avenging-take revenge for perceived wrong, defend, preserve, rescue</u>).

God ends this chapter with the second half of a promise he will fulfill when we call on Him, as stated in the previous verse. "…I will be with him in trouble; I will deliver him and honor him, with long life I will satisfy him and show him my salvation."

When we call on him, he comes on the scene. He will not leave us to face trouble on our own. He will equip us with a strategy and any material requirement to have victory over, or draw us out of the problem, altogether. He then honors us.

We learned yesterday that, "Honor speaks of heaviness in a good way. It is something that can be seen by others. It is rich and abundant. It is glorious in that it brings great happiness and thankfulness. It is a God promotion with tangible symbols signifying approval and distinction for us, with the added bonus of rewards and respect."

As if that was not more outstanding than we could imagine, he also gives us long life, satisfies us and shows us salvation. And this was written for people before they knew of Jesus.

Long life is just that, length of days. No explanation is needed here. But I can say that with this being a guaranteed promise from Almighty God, any ailment that comes knocking on our door, does so in direct conflict with the will of God. We need to stand firm against all things contrary to this word; anything that would attempt to thwart his promises being fulfilled in our life.

Satisfy means to sate. It means to fill to satisfaction, to have plenty of something. One of the definitions says it is the same as making a pig of oneself, overeating or stuffing oneself full. That is a picture of putting 6 pounds of sand in a 5 pound bucket. It is a picture of overflow. It is over-abundant supply confirmed time and time again in the Bible, and it is yours for the receiving.

Salvation does indeed mean to deliver, or save, or rescue, or preserve. It means defend or succor, giving assistance in time of difficulty or serious need. But it also means victory, prosperity, health, help, safety and welfare. You might remember from earlier studies; we have found that welfare is actually a good thing when coming from God.

But it is not good when it is coming in the form of long-term government assistance. There are some programs that have been contributed to for years and those benefits should have been managed properly and paid out to the contributor. And as a short-term stop-gap, it provides service, while a person gets back on their feet.

However welfare programs, on the whole, end up shacking the recipient into an inadequate lifestyle and a different category of slavery. It lowers expectations for a good life and hampers innovation in the recipient. Instead God's welfare is a contented state, one of being happy and healthy and prosperous. It is something that promotes enjoyment, happiness, health and prosperity.

Another interesting aspect of this word translated salvation, is that it is the Hebrew word is "Yeshua". Yeshua is Hebrew for Jesus. The aspects of the word salvation mimic in great part the definition of the word "shalom" that is so often translated "peace". It denotes an all-encompassing soundness, prosperity, health, peace and wholeness.

Although they are different words it is easy to see a parallel in meanings, and it also gives us insight into the saving grace of Jesus and the lifestyle He died to procure for us.

Good morning, Father. Thank you for not only the protection that this chapter tells us of, but the benefits received when we reach out to you; when we call on you. Although this was written before the work of Jesus that has given us the opportunity to be reconciled to you; this chapter once again points to the depth of the love, you have always had for your people. It points to your desire for our life of protected status, victory, happiness, recognition, health, and prosperity. You are the source of all things good and lovely in our lives, and we are learning more each day to receive all that you have set aside for us. We choose to accept an abundant supply, for the ability to give back to our families, communities and the world. We desire to do this because you placed the "want to" in us. We pray today for the peace of Jerusalem, for the protection and prosperity of our extended family, the Jewish people. Help us to operate in wisdom, we need your assistance to make proper decisions in our day to day life. In Jesus' name, we praise and thank you for it....Amen!

Definitions for today's study:
Long - from <H748> ('arak); length :- + **for ever**, length, long; a primitive root; to be (causative make) long (literal or figurative) :- defer, **draw out**, lengthen, (be, become, make, pro-) long, + (out-, over-) live, tarry (long).
Life - from an unused root meaning to be hot; a day (as the warm hours), whether literal (from sunrise to sunset, or from one sunset to the next), or figurative (a space of time defined by an associated term), [often used adverbially] :- age, + always, + chronicles, continually (-ance), daily, ([birth-], each, to) day, (now a, two) days (agone), + elder, × end, + evening, + (for) ever (-lasting, -more), × **full, life**, as (so) long as (...live), (even) now, + old, + **outlived**, + perpetually, presently, + remaineth, × required, season, × since, space, then, **(process of) time**, + as at other times, + in trouble, weather, (as) when, (a, the, within a) while (that), × whole (+ age), (full) year (-ly), + younger.
Satisfy - or sabea`, saw-bay'-ah; a primitive root; **to sate (fill to satisfaction)**, i.e. fill to satisfaction (literal or figurative) :- have enough, fill (full, self, with), be (to the) full (of), **have plenty** of, **be satiate [fill to satisfaction, overeat or eat immodestly or make a pig of oneself]**, satisfy (with), **suffice[be sufficient or adequate in quality or quantity]**, be weary of.

Shew - a primitive root; to see, literal or figurative (in numerous applications, direct and implied, transitive, intransitive and causative) :- advise self, appear, approve, behold, × certainly, **consider**, **discern**, (make to) enjoy, have experience, **gaze**, take heed, × indeed, × joyfully, lo, look (on, one another, one on another, one upon another, out, up, upon), mark, meet, × be near, perceive, **present**, **provide**, regard, (have) respect, (fore-, cause to, let) see (-r, -m, one another), shew (self), × **sight of others**, (e-) spy, stare, × surely, × think, view, visions.

Salvation - feminine passive participle of <H3467> (yasha`); **something saved**, i.e. (abstract) **deliverance**; hence aid, **victory**, **prosperity** :- deliverance, **health**, **help** (-ing), salvation, save, saving (health), **welfare**; a primitive root; properly to be open, wide or free, i.e. (by implication) to be safe; causative **to free** or **succor [assistance in time of difficulty or serious need]**:- × at all, **avenging [take revenge for a perceived wrong]**, **defend**, deliver (-er), help, **preserve**, **rescue**, be safe, bring (having) salvation, save (-iour), get victory.

111

Conclusion

Protection That Can't Be Beat

As a review of Psalm 91, I personalized it so that you can copy it off and put it on a card in your pocket. Your confession of His word over you and your family will strengthen your faith.

When I first came into the family of Christ this was one of the first chapters I memorized and said daily. I have mentioned before that my life was a mess back then and these verses helped me to feel protected.

Psalm 91 Daily Confession

1 I dwell in the secret place of the most High and abide under the shadow of the Almighty.

2 I will say of the LORD, He is my refuge and my fortress: my God; in him will I trust.

3 Surely You shall deliver me from the snare of the fowler, and from the noisome pestilence.

4 You shall cover me with Your feathers, and under Your wings do I trust: Your truth is my shield and buckler.

5 I am not be afraid for the terror by night; nor for the arrow that flies by day;

6 Nor for the pestilence that walks in darkness; nor for the destruction that wastes at noonday.

7 A thousand shall fall at my side, and ten thousand at my right hand; but it shall not come near me.

8 Only with my eyes do I behold and see the reward of the wicked.

9 Because I have made the LORD, my refuge, even the most High, my habitation;

10 There shall no evil befall me, neither shall any plague come near my dwelling.

11 For You give Your angels charge over me, to keep me in all my ways.

12 They shall bear me up in their hands, lest I dash my foot against a stone.

13 I tread upon the lion and adder: the young lion and the dragon I trample under feet.

14 Because I hath set my love upon You, therefore You deliver me: You set him on high, because I hath known Your name.

15 I shall call upon You, and You will answer me: You are with me in trouble; You will deliver me, and honor me.

16 With long life You satisfy me, and show me Your salvation.

This is the perfect book for someone you know who needs more understanding of who God wants to be for them.

Visit for more information 'Protection That Can't Be Beat' online at www.lindacnewberry.com

Yes, I want to give the gift of 'Protection That Can't Be Beat' to my friends and family.

	Quantity	Price Each	Subtotal
Protection That Can't Be Beat		$11.97	
		Shipping per book $5.00	
Please print legibly. Thank you!		Total →	

Name:_____

Address:_____

_____

Phone:_____

Email:_____

☐ MC   ☐ Visa   ☐ Discover   Exp. Date:_____

Card Number:_____

Signature_____

Tarshish Productions

1933 N Stone Maple Ln

Elkhart, IN 46514

www.lindacnewberry.com

bookinfo@lindacnewberry.com

Tarshish Productions

1933 N Stone Maple Ln
Elkhart, Indiana 47514

www.lindacnewberry.com
Info@lindacnewberry.com

www.ingramcontent.com/pod-product-compliance
Lightning Source LLC
Chambersburg PA
CBHW062000040426
42447CB00010B/1839